Barking Big

Barking Big

A Veterinarian's Inspiring
Story of Perseverance

Dan Castillo DVM

Copyright © 2021 by Dan Castillo DVM.

Library of Congress Control Number	2021906093
ISBN: Hardcover	978-1-6641-8276-9
Softcover	978-1-6641-8275-2
eBook	978-1-6641-8274-5

All rights reserved. No part of this book may be reproduced or transmitted in any form or by any means, electronic or mechanical, including photocopying, recording, or by any information storage and retrieval system, without permission in writing from the copyright owner.

Any people depicted in stock imagery provided by Getty Images are models, and such images are being used for illustrative purposes only.
Certain stock imagery © Getty Images.

Print information available on the last page.

Rev. date: 08/05/2021

To order additional copies of this book, contact:
Xlibris
844-714-8691
www.Xlibris.com
Orders@Xlibris.com
825317

Contents

Chapter 1	An Intracultural Union	1
Chapter 2	Young and Wild	11
Chapter 3	Opportunity Knocks	20
Chapter 4	Fears	24
Chapter 5	Dominican Justice, the Law of the Land	28
Chapter 6	Developing a Routine	30
Chapter 7	Hard Times	37
Chapter 8	Fate from a Phone Call	43
Chapter 9	Hard Work Pays Off	47
Chapter 10	One Roadblock after Another	52
Chapter 11	Just Keep Going	54
Chapter 12	Fight Mode	57
Chapter 13	Virginia—Great Experience but Tragic Times	64
Chapter 14	Going Back to Massachusetts	75
Chapter 15	The Art of No Money Down	80
Chapter 16	Ground Zero Shift, October 9, 2001	83
Chapter 17	Hold Your Cards Close	88
Chapter 18	Monopoly Money	96
Chapter 19	Life and Death Decisions	104
Chapter 20	Life Goes on at the Clinic	108
Chapter 21	Curbside Treatment—In the Era of COVID-19	113
Chapter 22	The Veterinary Industry, Corporate versus Private	114
Chapter 23	Good Debt versus Bad Debt	116

Chapter 1

An Intracultural Union

This book has been years in the making. Over the years, many people have told me I need to start documenting what I think and hope for all to read. It has been a pretty amazing journey. This book is a message for any parent, teacher, or mentor about what the possibilities are in any one individual. It is for any parent raising a kid who has lost his or her way or gotten sidetracked down the wrong path. There is always hope that this kid may find his or her own way.

Oddly enough, in the last couple of weeks, I just so happened to hear three famous individuals say what I believe are my own exact thoughts. Tom Brady in an interview by Howard Stern and Denzel Washington in a speech at a graduation said they had no plan B as far as their careers went. I am a veterinarian and have spent my whole life since the age of eighteen achieving this goal. They also said you need to fail—which I have many times.

Overcoming hurdles and failures and persevering in adversity are the most important skills we can have. I am constantly teaching this to my two sons, who are both in college, and to the interns and employees I have worked with over the last thirty years.

So let's start the journey of a very unique, unorthodox upbringing, education, and life.

First and foremost, my three sisters and I are the products of an intercultural marriage. I am Dominican and Irish, which is most unusual and was especially so back in those days. My parents were married in 1957. One would never look at my family and think that we had any Dominican blood. My dad and the Castillo family in the Dominican Republic are descendants of the Spanish founders of the country, and they are white. The Dominican Republic, or DR, is mixed with three races: Spanish from Spain, Taino Indian from the Caribbean, and black from the African slave trade. In the DR, this mix is called *mulatto*. The Dominican

Republic shares the island with Haiti, which I will not get into in too much detail. It is a history that is very complex, violent, and painful. To this day, there are major political issues between the two countries.

My mom is an Irish American from Staten Island, New York. Her family had lived in Staten Island for many generations. They did not migrate from Brooklyn after the construction of the Verrazano Bridge like many other families did. My dad migrated from the DR in 1955. He was twenty-seven. He was left fatherless at three years of age and raised by my grandmother, a single mom, and her sister and brother-in-law. My aunt and uncle never had children of their own, but they provided my dad, his sister (my aunt Ula), and his brother (my uncle Vincho) with a stable and loving home. My uncle Vincho was just born when his dad, my grandfather Peligrin Castillo, died in 1931. My dad and his siblings were also reared by a very large extended family of half brothers and sisters from my grandfather's previous marriage. As a matter of fact, those half brothers and sisters were about the same age as my grandmother. It is very common in Latin culture for multiple family members to raise and contribute to the entire family.

The history of my dad's family in the DR is very deep and began before the country's independence. My dad and his siblings were born at the beginning of the brutal dictatorship of Rafael Trujillo. He took power in 1931 and remained in power until he was assassinated in 1961. My family has endless stories about those times.

In the Time of the Butterflies is a book about the Mirabal sisters, who were killed during that time. One of them was a classmate of my uncle Vincho's. They spoke out and organized against the dictatorship and were eventually killed. This is one of thousands of stories that are real.

My dad's half brother Hostos was also murdered by the brutal regime. My dad talks about going to the funeral and hearing and seeing the very military officials who killed his brother there.

He described his time in medical school in the countryside. They called it *pasantia*. Medical students and residents spent time there treating the poor. My dad talked about how after long, hot days at work, he would go back to his housing and have dinner and then a few beers. One of the military officials who stood post would join my dad and the other medical students. After a few beers, the official would begin to break down and cry. He basically was dealing with post-traumatic stress disorder (PTSD) and depression. He would describe the brutality of holding babies on bayonets during the Haitian massacre in 1937, where Trujillo gave the order for ethnic cleansing. They called Trujillo "the Hitler of the West."

It was a different time. The Cold War was on, and he and every other dictator in Latin America was trained and supported by the United States. It is what it is and was what it was: tragic in every sense of the word. I heard a story about that time of a *New York Times* reporter trying to get information about the Haitian genocide. He was interviewing a Dominican military official. When the reporter asked the official about the killings, he responded, "No, there is no killing of any people here on the border." The reporter asked him again and again, and he repeated his denial.

Then the reporter finally said, "Sir! We have evidence of these killings of the Haitian people."

The official responded, "Oh, you mean the Haitians! Oh yes, we are killing them by the thousands."

What a mentality!

Just a side note: the relationship between these two countries, the Dominican Republic and Haiti, goes way back, and it is very complicated. But the issue now is simple. The DR is a poor country. It can no longer sustain the illegal immigration from Haiti. That needs to stop. For many in the international community, the easy fix for the problem is to make Haiti and the DR one country again. That will never happen. It would cause a major international crisis. Haiti is a sad situation; it has been abandoned, abused, and neglected. Maybe France and the international community could do a better job with a more proactive plan.

Let's get back on track. In 1955, Trujillo was sending doctors to the States with the intention of having them return. My father applied for a visa, but it didn't happen, despite many months, if not a year, of trying. My aunt, Tía Lela, just happened to be friends with Trujillo's brother Catano. After a phone call, my father's visa was granted in less than twenty-four hours. The family had his bags packed, and he was off to New York. I can't imagine that scene when he was leaving. It was done quickly, and the whole family was wondering whether his exit would be prevented. "When will he return?" was the big question. He said he knew he would only return if Trujillo was assassinated, which happened six years after he left.

The flight to New York was long. The first stop was Port-au-Prince, Haiti. My father walked into a bar, and the bartender looked at him with suspicion.

"What is your name, and where are you from?"

"I am from Cibao, the interior of the DR, San Francisco de Macoris. My last name is Castillo."

The bartender smiled and said, "I played baseball with your brother Hostos." He also mentioned how my family was a huge help to some of the Haitian people who worked the countryside. It was a crazy time. They called it the Parsley Massacre. If you couldn't say the word *peraril* (Spanish for parsley), you were murdered. There were times when my uncle Americo Castillo would hide someone in his trunk at a checkpoint. He was my dad's half brother and an attorney and governor with clout. The Castillo/Rodriquez family—my grandmother is a Rodriquez—are all influential attorneys.

My dad arrived in New York. His nineteen-year-old cousin who had married one of his classmates was there to greet him. He went to Manhattan and lived in a back room of an apartment. He once told me many of the doctors in that program came from all over the world but mostly Latin America. The doctors were recruited to hospitals all over the tristate area. One of the first hospitals he interviewed with was Staten Island Hospital. They offered him one hundred dollars a month and room and board. He was to specialize in psychiatry. Within a few weeks, he met my mom, who was a nurse's aide. She was very young at the time, about nineteen or twenty. The rest is history, folks. Lucy and Ricky, here we are. I think Desi Arnaz and Lucille Ball owe them a percentage of the *I Love Lucy* show's revenue.

The success of an intercultural or interracial relationship depends on love and support—period. The fact that the Stapleton family, a tough Irish New York family, took my dad in as one of their own is an example of what the entire world and this country should witness. Remember, this was in the 1950s. Most of my dad's colleagues who were darker skinned couldn't move around so easily. My dad's side also supported this intercultural marriage. He married *una gringa*, but they did nothing but shower us—my mom, my sisters, and me—with love and acceptance. We didn't know what they were saying, but we could sense the love and support. You don't get any more different than these two families, but together we are amazing. I am Castillo Stapleton. I will explain that later on in this book.

I was born in South Jersey, Vineland, in the little town of Anchora. My dad took a job with, I believe, the state of New Jersey. We were there until I was five. My memories there are pretty clear: Hamilton State Park, a large lake with freezing water and a large slide, and trips to Atlantic City and the beach, the Jersey Shore. We were all taught to swim and be comfortable around the water from a very young age. We were always with another family from the hospital or from Staten Island or the Dominican. We were raised pure American. I grew up with the song "O Danny Boy" constantly in the background. We never spoke Spanish in the house, although my mom did speak a little bit. It was the American way. The only time I heard Spanish was when my dad was on the phone talking with family or friends of his from upper Manhattan, Washington Heights. We didn't know what they were saying, but you could feel the closeness. They would hug you and kiss you and play games. It's a good learning lesson as well. Kids don't need to speak the same language; they just want to have fun.

For example, I remember my first trips to the DR. I was probably about five or so. On every trip, we were greeted by hundreds of family members. I would say on the plane, "Okay, get ready for the kissing machine." There they all were lined up, and we would walk the gauntlet. Our cousins in the Dominican didn't speak English. It didn't stop us from playing on the beach, riding horses on the farm, or playing dominoes or cards and making fun of each other trying to speak each other's language. The best times were fishing in Samana Bay, which is on the North Coast. It was crazy; we would all leave late at night in a boat and fish all night, catching everything, including shark. Mom would be praying all night until we returned. I would also bring down baseball equipment and play all day with the poor kids who spoke no English. It didn't stop us. My dad would ask that I leave all the equipment with them. It took a while to get used to, but eventually I understood it. The trips to the DR would be in the summer for about two to three weeks. That being said, we never spoke Spanish, and I never understood the language or the culture until I moved there at eighteen years of age.

Interesting how things come full circle. The town of Samana has been in our family for over a century. My grandfather was sent to jail there. He was a very influential attorney. His name was Don Peligrin Castillo. He also defended Trujillo, way before he was a dictator. Trujillo was accused of raising the Dominican flag during one of the occupations by the United States. There were multiple US occupations: 1916, 1924, and 1965. In 1965, there were forty thousand American troops in the Dominican Republic, more than there were in Vietnam. Trujillo requested my grandfather's service to defend him and asked him to plead his case. He did, and he won. At one time, he was sent to jail in Samana before the Trujillo regime, did six months there, and had a daughter, Celeste, my dad's half-sister. I am to this day so close to that extended family.

My father first went to Samana while my grandmother was suffering with malaria. A local doctor said it was best for her to recuperate close to the ocean breeze. She, my dad, and my aunt took the eighteen-hour journey by train, horse, and then boat. They lived there for six months. It was 1938, and he was nine years old. It was the first time he saw the ocean. Ironically, almost fifty years later, we would be performing spay and neuter clinics in that town. We have done so twice yearly since 1994 to this day. When my dad, aunt, and grandmother left for their journey, the youngest, my uncle Vincho, was left behind with the large extended family.

New York, Just Like I Pictured It, My Early Childhood in Ossining, New York

We moved from south Jersey to the town of Ossining, New York. It's about thirty to forty miles north of Manhattan. It's a beautiful town on the banks of the Hudson. It's where we would be schooled and raised from Brookside Elementary School, starting in kindergarten, to Anne M. Dorner Middle School, and finally Ossining High School. My young childhood was typical but somewhat isolated. We lived on the grounds of a major estate, Stony Lodge Hospital. It was a psychiatric facility. All the families of those who worked there, from the doctors to the maintenance employees and cooks, all grew up together. It was actually pretty awesome. That's all I really knew. It really wasn't being part of the community, like my family and I are now in the town of Franklin, Massachusetts. We did get involved with school things and other activities like Cub Scouts and Midget League Baseball, but we weren't part of a neighborhood. The hospital grounds were the neighborhood, and it was common to see severely mentally ill patients walking around, including Tennessee Williams's sister Rose. Williams was the writer of the classic book *The Glass Menagerie*. These were the patients of the time of lobotomies. That's why my motto until this day is "I'd rather have a bottle in front of me than a frontal lobotomy." Basically, it was a mental institution for the wealthy. It eventually developed. My dad's caseloads and specialty were with the youth, adolescents, and drug abuse.

Not being involved with the community or kids in the community, I believe has its drawbacks from a social aspect. For instance, I was never really involved with the town's recreation departments or youth sports. My social interaction was in school, with friends, in Cub Scouts, and during activities. I often wonder what makes a child or young adult choose a path or career or develop the will to fight and not give up. I think your interests start at a very young age. At least for me, they did. My parents were animal lovers. At one point, I think we had about twelve pets. We always had a dog, and we had cats, rabbits, Guinea pigs, hamsters, gerbils, and parrots. That was all at one time. This was my obsession and my interest.

I remember the one year I played Midget League (seven to eight years of age), we were in a game at a field at Brookside School. It was my turn to bat; I didn't hear anyone yelling my name. "Where is Danny?" My sister found me in the brook behind the field catching snakes and frogs. I was obsessed with the animals. The coaches were awesome. They knew I wasn't that good but worked with me. It's funny, years later, as a father, I was so connected in my community. I was so involved with all the sports programs. I coached many and actually was president of the Franklin Youth Lacrosse program, one of the largest lacrosse programs in the state. The Franklin Vet Clinic was converted into lacrosse central for about twelve years. Clients would bring in their pets and lacrosse equipment or checks or would want to talk to me or yell at me about why their kid wasn't getting more playing time. I would just say, "He needs to work harder," and then invite him to practice earlier to go over things. I was a ball buster as a coach, intense! You forget that these kids are like ten years of age. There was a time at U11 (age group under eleven years old) when the kids were playing in the hot sun. At halftime, the parents would bring oranges and things to keep them hydrated. The issue was they would lose total focus in the second half. So I had to lay the law down, no more oranges at the half. That didn't last too long, just until a parent yelled from the sideline, "Dan Castillo, give those kids something to drink." It was a great time. I really don't know how I did it all, running the practice at the same time.

Youth sports are great, but it did get out of hand as time went by, and it became more intense with the parents. I started coaching before my boys were old enough to play. They were four and five. I never got into it because of my boys. The lacrosse program was small back then.

I actually got involved by chance. I was working at the clinic, and a guy came in with a sheltie he had found walking down the highway. I didn't know the guy but assured him the dog was in good shape and had no ID tags on him. He asked if I could keep the dog for about two hours; he had to run and coach his kid for lacrosse. I mentioned that I had played in high school many years earlier. The rest is history. I showed up that day and just got more and more into it. The other coaches were like, "Who is this guy?" He doesn't even have a kid in the program. My boys grew up on the field and were involved in everything else, excluding football and hockey, which is pretty rare.

Lacrosse was our thing as a family. We traveled many miles and spent many summers in the tournament circuits up and down the East Coast. What's amazing is that the guy who brought that dog in many years ago is a very good friend of mine. All relationships that I have developed have come through my work at the practice. It may just be my personality. I'm very open and engaging with people. I not only ask about their pets but the owners themselves. I put myself out there. I'm just more personable than others. This is one reason why the practice has been successful.

At one time, while our kids were young, we were like many other families—spread too thin, jumping from one activity to another. At one point, we pulled the car over and realized this was not productive. The boys, Austin and Carter, would be changing uniforms, from Cub Scouts to baseball to karate. Cub Scouts was the first to go and then baseball. Karate, which we all did as a family, and lacrosse were their main interests.

As I mentioned, pets were my interest at a young age. Back in those days, the department stores would have a section dedicated to the pet store. That's where my parents would find me. At one point, my parents gave me ten dollars to buy school supplies with a friend's family. I ended up buying a hamster, the cage, and food at Barker's department store in Arcadian Shopping Center. My friend Michael's parents were shocked, as were my parents. It was something I wanted, so I got it. A great day for me would be going to the pet store and then having a slice of pizza at a place called Pizza Beat and ice cream at Baskin-Robins. That was a perfect day. They were all in the same center. It was also pretty common for my dad to come home from the city after seeing patients at his private office with a cat or two or even a parrot. The parrots would be smuggled in from the DR and sold in the streets of Washington Heights. Absolutely crazy.

I was also obsessed with two other things as a kid: music, specifically playing drums, and TV and movies. I started playing the drums at about eight years of age. I was heavily into it, with private lessons for about seven years. I was always involved with the band at school from elementary through middle school. It was pretty common for me to take my drums outside into my driveway and blast the music. I basically would play for the cars going by, and they would stop and watch. My parents supported it, even when our neighbors would complain. My mom would come out and say with her thick New York Staten Island accent, "Danny is going to practice his drums, you see."

The book I read most as a kid was the weekly *TV Guide*. I had it memorized. I was obsessed with *The Tonight Show* with Johnny Carson. I knew all the guests and would stay up late, sneak in, and watch. At one time, I convinced my parents that I should have a TV in my room. They actually put one in, and I was off. I loved all the shows: *The Partridge Family*, *Good Times*, and *The Brady Bunch*. I was completely obsessed. I would do imitations, basically steal them from Rich Little. *Kung Fu* was another show we were all crazy about. As kids in Brookside, all the boys would be practicing the kung fu moves.

I was a good student but always looking for a laugh. My dad would always say in his thick accent, "Danny, you need to apply yourself," "There is a time for work and play," or—this was a good one—"This year is the most important year." I was like eight years old. I would joke and make people laugh or try an imitation of John Wayne or Peter Falk in *Colombo*. It was mostly the quick things that came out of my mouth—shall I say no filter. For example, Mrs. Powers, our second-grade teacher, said, "Okay, kids, let's quiet down."

One classmate, Sarah, who is a teacher now, asked, "Doesn't kids mean baby goats?"

Mrs. Powers replied, "That is correct."

Without missing a beat, I said, "Hey, if we are the baby goats, you must be the old mother goat."

All laughed except for Mrs. Powers. "Okay, Danny Castillo, you will sit by my desk for the rest of the year."

I liked that. It was awesome. I liked all my teachers and would ask them about TV or movies. Many times, teachers would catch me daydreaming, looking out the window. They would say, "Danny Castillo, stop daydreaming," or would ask, "What are you thinking about?" I would tell them the truth. I'd talk about my new dog, a black Lab named Toro; my new drum set, a red sparkle Ludwig; or about a TV show. They would smile and say, "Okay, let's just focus on the lesson at hand."

At one time, for a while, I would miss the bus to go back home. Mr. McCarthy, who was the principal, would take me home. He was awesome. I would make him laugh, and he would listen to my stories. After about two to three days, it had to stop. My parents would say, "Make sure you don't miss the bus, or you will have no TV for three weeks." I think there was a discussion between Mr. McCarthy and my parents.

As we all graduated from Brookside, it was time to move on to the middle school. This is where things became a bit confusing. No more big fish small pond. It was sixth through eighth grade. It was tough. Kids were tough, better athletes, and you could get lost. The middle school was fed by the five elementary schools. One of them was Park School, which was downtown. It was the school of downtown Ossining, meaning it was Black / African American. I was always comfortable being exposed to Black people, vacationing in the DR, or going into Washington Heights with my dad on weekends to get a haircut or visit his friends. However, you learned to navigate things, to avoid things. For instance, don't make yourself seen. It wasn't unusual to have your lunch money taken or to need to fend for yourself—not just from Black kids but from anyone, it seemed. It was the early to mid-seventies with some racial tension. The fights were legendary, and the disruption in class at times was frequent. I focused on school and tried to do a good job.

The band was still my thing. As a matter of fact, the band leader heard about me and approached me to move up with the older kids after he asked me to read this music and play. I did, and I think he and the other students were like, "Okay, this kid's a player."

I started to meet kids from the other schools and other neighborhoods, from the other side of town, Nelson Park, Roosevelt, Claremont, St. Augustine's, and St. Theresa's. At times, I didn't lay low. My mouth got me into trouble, and I got my ass handed to me. For me, middle school is where I had the best teachers even to this day. One of my proudest moments in my entire career was going back to the same middle school and spending the entire day with my former science teacher, Joe Variano. It was an emotional time for the both of us but awesome. That was about fifteen years ago, and Joe and I still keep in touch. There was another couple of middle school teachers who had a major effect on me. One was Charles Hines. He was a Black teacher who didn't take shit from anyone and expected discipline. I was scared but worked my ass off. I started the first semester with a C; then I earned a B and then an A. He taught me to be prepared. Organize your notes and notebook. Don't ever be late, and study every day. Do not just cram for tests. He would give weekly quizzes, which made you prepare every day. I had a pretty good relationship with the middle school teachers. I worked hard and always made them laugh.

I was the movie critic too. Sundays were movie days with my family. We would travel as far as Stamford, Connecticut, to see a good movie. I was very young at the time to see things like *The Godfather Part II*, *Blazing Saddles*, *Bananas*, Woody Allen movies, *Papillon*, *Dog Day Afternoon*, and *The Sting*—classic movies. Teachers like Carl Oechner and Joe Variano would ask for my feedback. My bedroom was covered in posters of old movie classics, movie stars, and drummers like Gene Kruppa, Buddy Rich, and Louie Belson. I also of course had posters of animals, of the wild. I was into TV shows like Mutual of Omaha's *Wild Kingdom*.

The real fun started in middle school, especially the eighth grade. At that age, you feel a little more defiant and independent. You explore more. A memorable time was when a bunch of friends and I took our motorcycles on the trails way up in Yorktown to jump the trestles in the reservoir—Joe, Roger, Chris. It was magical really. You're on your own, all day, exploring and then getting the nerve to jump a fifty- to sixty-foot trestle in York Town, absolutely crazy. Given the shit we all did, we survived with the grace of God. That was all innocent back then.

Growing up in New York, I was much more used to being in a diverse society, which is awesome. I have been amazed through my travels how ignorant people are, not knowing what it is like to be exposed to people from all walks of life: Jewish, Italian, Irish, and Black. It was all there in Ossining, and for this, I am grateful and always proud of my New York heritage.

During the summers through elementary school and middle school, I vacationed either in the DR or in Cape Cod. So I was not around a lot in my hometown through the summer. We didn't go to camps or stay active in the community. I learned other things, like waterskiing, surfing on the Cape, and meeting other people. That was a good thing. The summer can be long, and being a parent raising two boys, I know if they are not busy or involved with something, there is too much time to get in trouble. For our family, lacrosse was our way of keeping busy. The boys were too young to work but old enough to get bored and get in trouble.

After the spring season, we would take the sport into the summer until mid- or the end of July. That meant practicing two to three times weekly at night and summer tournaments all up and down the East Coast.

As I have Zoom meetings with a group of high school classmates, I realize how fortunate I am to have them and to be reconnecting with them through social media. I know how negative social media can be, but the positive thing, at least through Facebook, is it has reconnected me with friends that I have known since I was five years of age. It is pretty awesome. The reconnection started at about the tenth-year reunion. We are now preparing for our fortieth. It's funny; at the ten-year reunion, everyone seems to be in their own world and somewhat competitive. As you reach the twentieth and thirtieth, that all falls by the wayside. Most have kids and their own families and seem to be much more grounded. It is more genuine. Speaking or texting with most, you sense that it is genuine closeness and caring about one another and their families.

Chapter 2

Young and Wild

My high school years were tough, regretful, and all fun at the same time. Too much fun was my issue. I just couldn't seem to settle down. As fellow Ossining High students read this, they may completely disagree. One would ask, in my high school in a class of about 420 students, how can some go to Harvard or MIT and others go to jail or not even graduate? If you were caught somewhere in the middle like me, I can explain and give you my opinion.

Too much freedom! It was an open campus, which meant you could come and go as you wanted. Upperclassmen with cars were in and out all day. There were students doing drugs and drinking openly on campus, and there was violence. Things were settled violently with fights. When I went back to my middle school about fifteen years ago for career day, my former teacher Joe Variano, who was very active in the school system and also coached in the high school, said, "Danny, your class of 1980 and two years before and maybe one year after were the most violent." Friday-night hockey games often ended in a brawl. An issue in the cafeteria or in class would end in a brawl. It was always something. So what makes one kid avoid all the bullshit and another get drawn into it? Not being involved in anything and having too much time on one's hands is the main cause.

My first mistake of many was listening to an upperclassman. He convinced me to drop band. It was the biggest mistake. The band leader heard about me, but what I saw was having A, B, and C lunch off, which was from about 11:00 a.m. to 1:30 p.m. I don't want to glorify the things I got into, but it's important to talk about. I was first introduced to pot at about the age of eleven or twelve by a cousin of mine in Staten Island. Not good at all. As far as drugs are concerned, you name it, it was all over. I would like to leave it at that and not get into too much detail.

The first day of my freshman year, I walked in and was called over by a friend of a friend. They were smoking. Two weeks into the ninth grade, my parents took my older sister Gilda to college in Boston, to Northeastern. I stayed back and started the day playing the drums in the driveway. I ended up taking my mother's car and joyriding all day with groups of friends. I eventually got caught by my neighbor, Dr. Basmaci. I tried to bullshit my way out of it and say the car was at the mechanic's all day. He was my dad's colleague and said, "Danny! I just saw you driving the car." I denied it until I broke down and cried. Petty crime was common for me. I was pressured by upperclassmen. One was named Bobby. He protected me in a lot of ways, but it was trouble. I would shoplift albums, and then he would sell them with his friends. It went on and on. My grades were poor.

A group of friends and I got caught smoking pot. A cop pulled up right behind us as we were on the hill at the high school. The cop's son actually sold us the stuff. The politics and bullshit never stops. A good friend got caught or was the only one chosen to get in the car and go to the principal. He is a very good friend to this day. He was able to turn the ship around and completely avoided all the bullshit. He was a phenomenal athlete. I, in contrast, was not and was into hanging out and partying. I was a late bloomer, as they say. In the ninth grade, I was five feet three inches and 103 pounds. In the tenth grade, I was five feet six inches, maybe 120 pounds. I graduated high school about maybe five feet eleven, and now I am six feet two inches and a pretty good athlete.

When I was implicated in my friend getting caught along with the others, I had to go see my father in his office. As I was walking in through the hospital grounds of Stony Lodge, it seemed all the employees knew what had happened and just gave me a look of "Holy shit! Doc's kid is in trouble."

My dad basically said, "If you want to smoke reefer, go ahead, but if the cops pick you up, you're on your own. Don't come to me."

My dad worked with adolescents in trouble with the law, drugs, and mental issues. When he was on call for the hospital, he would get a call saying one of the kids escaped from the hospital and was locked up in jail. I would hear him tell the parents, "No, don't bail him out tonight. Let him spend the night in jail and think about it. I straightened out a bit but not really. I hit the tenth grade. I did a little better but not much. The summer of my tenth-grade year, going into the eleventh, I decided not to go to the DR. I wanted to hang around town, so I got a job with the rec department of Ossining and worked as a janitor at the middle school. This was not a good idea. Now I had time and money. It was a learning experience.

I remember the crew that I worked with very well—one guy specifically. He was a Black man named Harvey and a Vietnam vet. He once gave me a job for the morning, which was cleaning the bottoms of garbage cans and then mopping. I gave him a little attitude, and he stopped me cold in my shoes and had a real sitdown with me about discipline, respect, and listening to orders. He showed me the correct way to mop. Even now, at the practice, I show all newcomers how to mop and then have to tell the story of Harvey. He also started to ask about my last name, Castillo, pronounced with the "yo," not as in the Brillo pad. I explained I was half Dominican but said it with some shame or embarrassment. I don't know why, but I did. He again stopped me dead cold and said, "Danny, don't ever feel ashamed of who you are and where you are from. Look what your dad did coming to this country. You're a doctor's son. Work hard, and be proud." Harvey was awesome, and I will never forget him.

Junior year was not great at all. I was too much into hanging out and partying. I would work at Stony Lodge doing odd jobs on the weekends—dishwashing was a tough deal. This meant my weekends were booked with work, which did not go well. I went out real late one Saturday night and decided to sleep in and not show up to work early Sunday morning. My dad walked in and said, "Get up, and get out of bed. People are waiting for you to go to work. You need to show up and be accountable." He basically told me to get the hell out of bed and not to be late. It was a long day washing dishes hungover, to say the least. I was seventeen years old. Junior year is when you need to strive for grades and do the best possible, as you are prepping for the SATs and the college application process. The amount of work my wife, Ellen, and I did and the amount of money we spent prepping our boys with tutors and coaches were amazing. It did pay off. We were so much more involved with the boys than my parents were with me. Maybe it was the times; maybe it was just me.

The night before the SATs, I was out until late at night partying. I don't even remember studying for them. It was a complete disaster. I took them again, and it was even more of a disaster. I received a 200 in math and a 300 in English. Yes, that is correct—a 200 and 300! When I repeated the exam, I received the exact same grade: a 300 in math and a 200 in English. I think you receive a 200 for just filling out the form. This is nothing to brag about or hide. It is what it is. That's where I was, but I was going to an even tougher place.

Toward the end of my junior year, I was doing pretty well in lacrosse. I got the most improved award. It was the first award I ever received. I got into lacrosse in the ninth grade. I was walking with a friend of mine across campus when I saw these two guys running and shooting on a goal. I couldn't believe what I was watching. One of the players was exceptional. His name was Doug Saltzman. He was amazing. Unfortunately he was killed on his motorcycle in his freshman year of college while visiting home. Since then, they have given out the MVP in Doug's name. I think of him very often and pray for his family. What a tragic loss. I think of all the time my family has dedicated to this sport and know watching Doug that first day was a huge factor. My boys were not only captains of their high school teams, but my youngest is playing at the college level at the University of Massachusetts (UMass) Amherst.

The summer of my junior year, things took a very bad turn. I was introduced, and in some cases reintroduced, to a group of guys for whom, at the time, I would have run though a brick wall. I haven't seen or heard from any of them in over thirty years. It was a tough run, living on the edge and one party after the other. If they had given out grades or awards, I would have gotten straight A's. I had it all figured out—the bars and the hangouts in town, Roosevelt Square, Brookside school, Campwoods, the train station, Nelson Park, the river. I was up all night partying and having my friends drop me off right to work at 7:00 a.m. for landscaping at Stony Lodge. It was a disaster. My biggest hangout was Veterans Park. It was right down the street from where I lived, 15 Grand View Ave. I actually visit there while I am visiting my old neighbors I grew up with, Dianne and her husband, Vinny. The first time, about two years ago, I drove through the park and had somewhat of an overwhelming feeling; it wasn't a real good feeling to be honest. I caused some problems back then, but at the same time, I had a lot of fun as well.

I was almost killed twice in the span of nine months while entering and leaving my senior year. It was August 25, 1979. I was seventeen, and my friend Scott had his eighteenth birthday. The party started at noon and ended with me, him, and two others, John and Tommy, going head-on with a tree at 4:00 a.m. off of Stormy Town Road in Ossining. Scott was driving; I was in front and the other two in the back. All of us ended up in the hospital except for Scott, the driver. It was horrible. We were flying around, jamming brown sugar, and thank God, I was awake and saw the tree coming while going off the road. I put my body down toward the driver seat as if to duck away. The crash was all in on my side. I could have easily been incapacitated. I ended up in the hospital for about three days, with my arm almost ripped off from a tree branch and a concussion. I remember being cut out of the car and my friend John saying, "Dan, you're fucked up." I was in complete shock. I remember my mom and John's mom crying over us. It was a bad situation. Thank you, God, for saving me.

A week later, I was entering my senior year with dark sunglasses to hide my facial bruising and a sling for my arm. I remember going to gym and the teacher / coach saying, "Danny, take the sunglasses off. Where do you think you are?" I took them off. He saw my eyes and said, "It's okay. You will be all right. Put them back on."

Judy Berehns was one of my favorite English teachers in middle school. She moved to the high school and saw me all beat up. She was so good. She said, "Danny, what is going on? What are you doing? Are you going to college?" I really had no plan. She knew my parents and said, "They must be so upset." I almost felt like crying in her arms.

You would think that a traumatic episode like this would scare the life out of me. It didn't! I just kept going with the same old BS. As a matter of fact, I kept getting in the same car and hanging with the same crew. There is nothing wrong with these guys, and I know from what I have been told some have their own families. If I saw them, I would hug them and have a beer. We all know we are lucky to have survived our youth.

The end of my senior year was not any better; my lacrosse season was average, nothing major. I was dealing with a back issue, and I wasn't able to compete as much. We had some very athletic juniors from the class of 1981. About three weeks before my graduation, I was hanging out with the group of geniuses when words were passed back and forth with a group of guys from the next town over, Croton, New York. One of my friends poured a beer on a guy's Mustang. All was good. Nothing happened. We went home and called it a night.

About a week later, I was at the same bar, Gallagher's, with another good friend of mine, Chip. It was a Wednesday night, and we were watching the Yankees game. We were talking about how weeks before I and two other guys almost drowned in Silver Lake in Croton. I will get into that story later. We went outside to get some air. While I was standing and facing Chip, a guy and his friend slammed me over the head with a beer mug—a major haymaker. I did not see it coming and had no way to block it or avoid it. I slammed to the ground. The term *fight or flight* is real. Your adrenaline kicks in. I hit the ground and ran as fast as I could with blood covering my face and entire body. I ran into the bar across the street. The patrons and the bartender were completely freaked out. I was screaming for help. People were frozen. The bartender eventually yelled out, "Get you and your blood out of here!" It was a horrible situation. The cops came and took me to Phelps Memorial Hospital, where they placed about twenty stiches. Glass was all in my head, and it took a long time, hours. My friend basically took me home with a turban bandage around my entire head. It was a horrible scene at my house. My dad was trying to throw me out, calling me a bum, and my mom was crying. I was in complete shock and had PTSD. I literally had no clue what just happened.

A week or so after this trauma, I was with a group of friends heading up to the cliffs in Croton. We saw the car of the guy who assaulted me and vandalized it. Of course we got caught and were called down to the state troopers' office in Peekskill, New York. Things were just out of control. Nothing happened with us; we just had to pay for damages. Nothing happened with the assault charges either. It happened to be that the kid was the son of a town of Croton constable. I did go to court and saw him and his family there. I was alone. My family wanted nothing to do with it. It was a horrible situation. I would see the kid and his friends all summer, and fights would start in the same bar where it all happened—Gallagher's in Croton. Back then, the drinking age was eighteen, and that was the culture.

I showed up to our last lacrosse game of the season—and for me, my career—unable to play. I was still in shock with a turban bandage around my head. Coach Pritts was so disappointed; he had known me since elementary school and was speechless. I was a lost cause. My mother came into my room that next day and said, "You are going to get killed. Why are you doing this?" It was a very tough time. I was graduating in two weeks and had absolutely no plan on what I was going to do.

I have connected with a friend from way back in the day who was with me during those tough years of our youth. We have not seen each other since the mid-eighties. We occasionally text. He has done very well for himself as a restaurateur in Arizona and has made quite a name for himself. I saw him give a keynote speech at a convention regarding his profession. When he spoke a bit about his hometown of Ossining and his youth, he got choked up. I texted him. I knew what he was choked up about. We survived, worked our asses off, and made a name and career for ourselves. It could have been a lot different. We got lucky, worked very hard, and with the grace of God survived. He was in a bad situation as a freshman when at the same Veterans Park, he was talked into drinking a gallon of burgundy wine. He passed out cold, basically alcohol intoxication. I lived the closest, so I ran home and called his family. I spoke to his brother. They were down in a second and off to the hospital. Thank God he survived.

The night of my graduation, my family and I all went out for dinner. I can't believe to this day, my parents didn't really have a plan on what to do with me. There was a plan to go to Westchester Community College and even a possibility of joining the air force. My mom's family in Staten Island were pretty well known in the union for the printing press for the *New York Times*. My mom was from more of a blue-collar background, which was great. Her suggestion for me was to take a civil service test and get into a union—police, fire department, or US postal service, where one of my uncles, Vince Palladino, was a very well-known figure. All positions were good, but none interested me at the time. My main goal was finishing dinner and getting to a graduation party.

It did start to bother me that most friends I knew or grew up with were all planning to leave in September. One friend got into Rochester Institute of Technology (RIT) and had no business going there. His dad had a connection. He was a student like me. It just goes to show with the right connection, something can happen. The fact is that my friend lasted a semester. You need to work your ass off and have the ability to take advantage of your opportunity.

During dinner, one of my sisters asked, "So, Dan, what is your plan now?"

I was stunned but mumbled some BS. My dad jumped in and said, "Hey, I can send you to Santo Domingo, and you can take your time on what you think you may want to do."

I jumped at the opportunity. I basically wanted to go to the party and say I had a plan, and I was leaving in September as well. Dinner was done, and I couldn't get to the party quick enough with my news. This is where my life was about to change, and I eventually would turn things around with a lot of work, heartache, and failure.

At the party, I ended up seeing a friend I had known for quite a while. We actually started to date and were very close. She was a very important influence, looking back, and I have let her know. She actually settled me down for that summer and the years through college. It's pretty awesome; she's married to a great guy and has kids of her own. Her importance and influence will come later on at some difficult times.

As I am writing this on June 10, 2020, our country is suffering with the pandemic and racial tensions with the killing of George Floyd in Minnesota. I have to look back in my youth at racial tensions in Ossining. Was Ossining a racist town? I don't think so. Did Ossining have some ignorant people like everywhere else in the world who passed that ignorance down to their children? I would say yes. Let's review some things that I witnessed and things that have happened to me and my family personally. In no way, shape, or form would I classify my looks or heritage as making me a target, but I'll let you make that decision.

A year before I entered the high school, there was a riot that made the news all over. Was it a fight or a riot? Well, it was between Blacks and Whites.

At Veterans Park, a Black kid and White kid had a basketball game. It ended up in a verbal fight with the White kid screaming as the Black kid walked down the hill to the parking lot, "Nigger, when you get some money, come uptown and play again!" Words were exchanged back and forth— Nigger, Honkey. Is this racist?

Veterans Park was a big hangout. One night, when I was a freshman, an upperclassman drove up. His window had been smashed in with a brick as he was driving through downtown. He gathered at least twenty guys to go downtown and retaliate against the Blacks. "Let's go burn some crosses." Ignorance or true racist?

There was always one issue going regarding that. However, there may be a fight, and then you would see them all hanging out the next day. It's how it was done.

For me, personally, I was in the fifth grade, and Mrs. Carr, who was a very good teacher but hard, was giving out little books to the students about their heritage so they could do a huge report in the next week. There were books about Ireland, Israel, Poland, and Italy. We had kids from all over. There was a book about Puerto Rico. She said, "Here you go, Danny."

I was like, "Okay, awesome."

Well, I took the book home, and my dad was like, "What is this?" He was not happy and said, "You take this book back and tell her we are not Puerto Rican."

My sisters were supportive ... Yeah, right! They were like, "You idiot, we are Dominican and Irish." Long story short, I was too afraid to tell my teacher and never handed the report in but said I did hand in the report and they must have lost it. Racist? No, just not informed about my heritage, and I was too young or afraid to explain.

I was about ten years old, and my younger sister Mimi was eight. We were walking up Grandview, and one of the neighbor's kids taunted us face to face, as he was walking backward, "You spic, you guys are smelly spics, you fucken' slobs."

I was telling Mimi, "Just keep walking, Mimi. It will all be okay."

When we got to the top, we went home. My other neighbor Roy saw I was upset. He walked down the hill, got ahold of the kid, and slapped his ear from one side of his head to the other. As the kid was lying there in shock and pain, Roy said, "You touch him again, you're fucking dead." That's how things were settled. A couple of years later, the kid who was saying this to us said it to the wrong guy, a very good friend of mine named Joe. He was Cuban. Joe was much bigger and stronger and beat him to a pulp against a backstop while his dad watched. While the kid was beaten and bloodied on the ground, Joe looked up the hill and said, "Dad, did I do enough?" and his dad responded, "You didn't show me nothing yet," in his thick Spanish accent.

In 1980, during the Mariel boatlift, Castro unleashed all his jails and let the unwanted from Cuba hit the shores of Miami, and then President Jimmy Carter welcomed them with open arms. Just watch the movie *Scarface* with Al Pacino. We were all hanging at a friend's house, and my friend's mom went off on the spics coming to this country. A group of friends started to look at me. As we were pulling out of the driveway, the mom came running out apologizing and was horrified. My friend who was driving on the way home was like, "Dan, you okay?"

"I am fine, no worries."

Racist, ignorant?

In 1980, Hurricane David ravaged the Dominican Republic. My dad asked us to gather boxes of clothes and material to send to the DR. He was upset. We would take the supplies to Washington Heights. I told the story to friends. It became the brunt of many jokes that even I laughed at. I didn't realize the devastation until I went down there to live. They had no running water for months, and my grandmother was dealing with pancreatic cancer at the time. You don't understand things until you live it.

I am a white boy, as American as they come. I had family who fought and died in World War I, World War II, and Vietnam. I came from a hardworking, typical American family. I was raised American. As a little kid, you think it's normal that your dad has family and friends visiting and you attend parties or barbecues in the backyard speaking Spanish. I guess neighbors may have seen it differently. Most if not all of the people I grew up with thought I was Italian up until I left for the DR.

As a little boy and through middle school, I would go into Washington Heights with my dad to pick up friends or family and visit. I was blond-haired and white, and people would be saying with a Spanish accent, "Why don't you speak Spanish? How do you talk to your family in the DR and your grandmother?" Some would almost have an attitude against me or would be in shock. I would respond, "I don't need to speak Spanish. My family in the Dominican just hugs me and kisses me all day."

The summer of my graduation passed, and as friends started to leave for college, I was ready to go. The plan was to go to the DR, come back in December, and most likely go to Westchester Community College. I was brought to Kennedy Airport and hopped on Dominicana Airlines. It went out of business years ago. I was very carefree about it because my plan was to return anyway. I could tell this was going to be some trip right at Kennedy. I boarded the plane, and the party started. The entire plane was Dominican; they were drinking rum, playing music, and all talking and laughing, and I had no clue what was happening. I did start to get a little nervous. When my parents dropped me off, I think they were a little relieved I was leaving.

Chapter 3

Opportunity Knocks

My two cousins picked me up in the DR with open arms and smiles. However, this was different; it wasn't vacation mode or beach mode. As a matter of fact, we were able to communicate but with much difficulty. My family in the DR does not speak one word of English. I was able to get by and was brought to my aunt Ula's condo. Aunt Ula is my dad's sister. She was living there with their aunt and uncle who raised them, Tia Lela and Tio Ciqui (Enrique). My grandmother had passed away months before in May of that year. I spent those months hanging out basically doing nothing. The key point was that all my family—aunts, uncles, and multiple cousins—would ask, "What are you going to study? Medicine? Law?" My family from the DR are all attorneys. That goes back for centuries. My uncle Vincho is a very influential attorney and politician, and his three sons and daughter are all attorneys. My dad and another cousin of mine are doctors.

One didn't just go to college and think about what one wanted to do. It was the European system there. The university was a five-year plan with two years of basic classes and then courses geared toward your major. So right after high school, you entered the university with a major. In my family, the major was law or medicine. I spent the next three months meeting and talking with many family members and friends of family members who were all either students in the university or professionals—doctors, lawyers, or engineers. I met an American student who lived upstairs from my aunt. She was named Denise and was from Long Island. She went to undergrad in the States and was attending veterinary school at the same university all my cousins went to, La Unphu, Universidad Nacional Pedro Henrique Urena. Sounded good to me. I would go upstairs and talk to Denise, and I met multiple other students from the States studying with her. All were much older than I was, late twenties and thirties. I was only eighteen at the time. They were students who either didn't get into vet school in the States or couldn't afford it. I eventually met a student from New Jersey named Chris. He was more like me. He was half Dominican and half Greek, born and raised in New Jersey, but very fluent in Spanish. He had spoken Spanish in the house as a kid, unlike my family. Chris was different; he wasn't like the other students. He entered the vet school at the university right after high school.

After months of discussions with my family, the subject continued on what my plan was. I talked about going to Westchester Community College or working at the GM plant in Tarrytown, New York. They emphasized the importance of school and education and having a profession or a career. By November, after a social gathering with so many family members and so many friends of family, seeing Denise and Chris, and meeting other vet students, both American and Dominican, I brought up with my cousins and family that I had always wanted to be a veterinarian. It was either that or a drummer, an actor, or a movie critic. They all laughed at the actor and movie critic. They would mention and emphasize that the most important years that may dictate your destiny are from eighteen to twenty-five—not totally, but what you do at that time is key. I started to talk to Chris and the other students. Chris's take was start now, like he did right after high school. The other older students were more on the side of going to college in the States first to grow and mature and make sure that was what I really wanted to do.

One night, most of my large family was at a gathering, and we started to talk about my thoughts about being a veterinarian. The idea of being a veterinarian struck them all as odd. The profession at least back then in that country was that of a large animal vet, working on the farms. It made no sense to them, as the culture was different. However, they were all supportive and were all like, "Okay, let's get you enrolled. The idea of going back to the States and going to college in their minds was crazy. They said, "Go now. Enter now while you can." Then this topic came up as I mentioned to them, "I cannot be a veterinarian. I don't have the grades to become a vet. It is way out of my reach and a complete impossibility." They were all amazed and shocked at my attitude. "What do you mean you can't do something you want?"

I would try to explain to them that my guidance counselor in high school said I couldn't. I didn't have the grades to get into one of the hardest careers ever. It was and is harder to get into vet school than medical school, being that there are only twenty-eight vet schools in the entire United States, and the competition is grueling. It's not for everybody. My family would not accept anyone ever telling anyone they couldn't achieve anything they wanted. That was unacceptable and negligent. How could a kid from Ossining Public High School with this background, SAT 200 and 300, GPA 74.6, class rank #364 of what I remember as a class of 424, make it anywhere, let alone doing it all in another language? The chances of success were between slim and none. The chances were *zero*. I would say things like, "I am not good in math. I hate math. How can I ever do it?"

Their response was, "Well, they are going to give you the material, and you are going to sit down and study it and pass. If you don't do well, you will try again and then pass." Believe it or not, by December, my third month living in the DR, I was able to communicate much more easily. I was definitely better at understanding the language than speaking it. So that December, I had my ticket to return to New York and spend the holidays. I would tell my family the news about me planning to enter veterinary school the following year. I basically took a gap year.

I was back in New York from December to March and then returned to the DR to take some Spanish lessons from a teacher in the condo unit. She was good, but she was amazed at my basic grammar. That grammar did come from Gail Litchenstein, my Spanish teacher in high school. The best Spanish lesson was just living it. Remember, this was 1980—no internet or cable. I was completely immersed. I returned to New York on December 10.

Something I would never forget happened a couple of days before my trip. We were at a red light, and one of the poor Dominican paperboys had a headline, "Mataron a John Lennon." My cousins were all speaking in Spanish. I really didn't understand until I heard the name John Lennon. He was killed on December 8. It was hard. Even in the Dominican Republic, you could see the sadness and almost fear.

I landed at Kennedy, and my dad picked me up. I broke the news of my plan. We stopped over in Washington Heights to see his friends. It was then I realized how much I was missing when all were talking Spanish. I finally was able to understand the conversations. I could not yet talk, but I could understand for sure. It was pretty awesome. The group was all talking about what everyone else talks about: their kids, politics, and of course baseball and current events. My dad was excited about my plan to go to school in the DR. Everyone else, including my mom, was like, "What? You're going back and doing what?" It was quite a shocker for all. My friends in Ossining were dumbfounded. Most, including family members, thought it would be a short trip. I most likely wouldn't make it.

I spent the next three months from December to March prepping with a math tutor at Stony Lodge, but mostly I was, as my dad would say, up to my old tricks again. It was one big major party in Ossining.

I retuned in March to the DR and returned to Ossining in June of 1981. It was a great summer. I was with my girlfriend and hanging with my friends. It was awesome until the summer was drawing to an end. As we reached August, I started to get real nervous. When we hit mid-August, she was off to college, and I was off to what I had been talking about for the last year. I became overwhelmed, saying goodbye to her and everyone else, my family and friends. I would lose it at times. I remember heading up to a park with her to say goodbye to her family. I believe it was a family reunion and a going-away party for her as well, as she was about to leave for college later that week. We were sent to get some supplies at her house, and I remember completely losing it with tears. She asked that I get it together, as we needed to head back to the party at the Gerlach Park down by their house.

As we exited the car, it was obvious that I was upset. As I made my rounds, saying goodbye to all, it was almost unbearable. Her mom was awesome. She took me aside and said, "Study hard, Danny. You can do whatever you want. Just study and work hard." She hugged me, and I didn't want to let go. She was the only person who said something like that to me at that time. Not even my own family gave me that advice. Most people were thinking, *What the hell is he doing, and where is he going? He will never make it. There is no way he will be able to pull this off. Go to college in a completely different language?* The fear, doubt, insecurity, and reality were hitting me like a ton of bricks. I was off and ready to start on August 17, 1981. My ID number was 81-0395. I would be officially called Castillo Stapleton. You are known by your last name and your mother's maiden name. I also started to pronounce my last name the correct way, Castillo with "yo," not "illo," like the Brillo pad.

I have to pause for a minute and make it clear I am not being critical of my high school or my guidance counselor. There were good ones and not-so-good ones. I was not a good student. There is no argument there. The teachers and counselors have just so much to work with, numbers, stats, and other factors. However numbers, like ranking and SAT scores, are so important. We spent so much time with our boys and money achieving those goals. My boys have been outproducing me in every respect. The irony is now in this pandemic, there is a discussion about discontinuing the SAT.

Chapter 4

Fears

If I were to describe my first two years in vet school living in the DR or at least the first eighteen months, I would have to say I felt deep sadness, loneliness, isolation, complete shell and culture shock, and of course major *fear* and homesickness. I also believe I was suffering from a little PTSD. The trauma of a car accident and getting assaulted all in my senior year was a bit much. I remember having dreams of falling a lot and not landing and then waking up in a panic. That was also combined with the whole new change of living in a different country away from all that I knew. I lived in the spare bedroom at the house of my aunt and my grand-aunt and uncle, who were in their eighties. I didn't realize that this room would be my place for the next five or six years. There was no dorm life or college life. My family did everything for me. They provided food and comfort, cleaned my clothes, basically just took me in as one of their own. It's hard to imagine something like this happening in the States. Maybe it does, but I can't imagine my sister sending one of my nephews to my home for five or six years.

I could barely speak a full sentence in Spanish, and I was about to report to class at 7:00 a.m. My aunt let me borrow her car at times, but other times, I needed to take *un carro publico*, a public car packed with about ten people and not smelling too good. I arrived at the school with my heart in my stomach, walked into the class, and almost fainted. The other students just stared at me with awe, as I was the only tall and white guy they had probably ever seen. I tried to focus, and as the teacher started to speak, I could feel the earth shake. He shouted, "Que esta pasando?" (What is happening?) It was a grade-4 earthquake, a tremble. People ran like a stampede to the parking lot. I guess they say it's not uncommon in the summer months with the heat.

It was frustrating. There was not one thing I liked about it. I had no friends, no one to talk to, and no one to hang out with day after day. I would go back to my aunt's house for lunch. Lunch is the primary meal in the DR and Latin America. I would eat in the heat, look across the table at the old people, and almost burst out crying. We would go off to our rooms, and I would cry until I had to go back to school at 2:00 or 3:00 p.m. and stay until about 6:00 or 7:00 p.m. When I would return at night, I would have a light dinner, go off to my room, and literally break down to the point of hyperventilating.

I had a cousin from Queens. Alfred Castillo; his father and my dad are like second cousins. I didn't meet him until he moved to the DR at the same time I did. He was staying with another aunt. Alfred was studying medicine. After all these years of practicing, he is in the middle of the COVID pandemic in Queens. His mom was from Spain, so he spoke Spanish fluently. We became and still are like brothers. We saw each other occasionally and just talked about home and being back in the States. We both had calendars in our room that we would check off daily. One has to remember, the world was very large back then. There was no cable or internet, and no one spoke English. For me to call home, it would have to be after 11:00 p.m. I would have to connect with about two different operators. When I talked to my family, it seemed like they were a million miles away with a lot of static.

Things did not get easier. On my first biology test, I got a sixteen! Some of the older American students that I would see around campus couldn't believe it. They were all saying I needed to go back to college, grow up, and learn how to study. They were right, but I marched on with no plan B. I talked to my biology teacher. She knew I had no clue and didn't understand the language. She arranged to meet with me on Saturdays. I worked harder, repeated the test, and got a seventy-five. I worked, and she gave me a chance. I ended up passing with a C, and I took it with joy. One has to realize that all of my classes were in Spanish, including organic chemistry, pathology, anatomy, and every other class, including math.

My family was always there for me. They would see the frustration, and with a lot of encouragement, they would just tell me to keep going and work harder. As time went on, it was all still difficult, but it started to become routine. I started to get involved with fitness activities, working out, running, biking. At times, I would grab on to a platano truck while on my bike and cross Santo Domingo city traffic to Hotel Lina about eight miles away. I'd work out at the gym and ride back at night. Lucia, our maid, would have dinner for me and a big pot of café Santo Domingo to keep me up all hours to study. She would also get the candles or kerosene lamp ready, as the blackouts would happen almost all the time. For the first year and a half, I would take a little tape recorder to class and then play it back at night and try to take notes in Spanish. My writing and understanding of the language came first, before I could actually speak it. Then I just had to speak without being too nervous or uncomfortable. There was no way I could even engage with anyone. I was asked to read in front of class at times, which was frightening.

I mentioned Lucia, the maid. In the DR, "maid" is not the correct phrase. Down there, it's part of *el servicio*. In our family, the maids, bodyguards, and chauffeurs have been in the family for twenty, thirty, or forty years. They are all like family members. Lucia was such a big part of my life. So was her son Miguel. He was a little boy back then. I used to practice my Spanish, and Miguel used to try to dance like Michael Jackson. Physical fitness was my savior. I started taking tae kwan do and working out at a medical student's house. Fernando had his entire backyard converted to a gym literally under a hot tin roof. This was what I needed to do to escape the stress and loneliness, and it made me feel better. Also, almost everyone I met was a student in either medicine, law, business, or engineering. I was surrounded by that environment.

I also got more involved with my family as far as politics. My uncle Vincho campaigned in 1982 and 1986, and I spent much time on the trail, Latin American style, with all the bodyguards and marches and of course death threats. It would not be uncommon for the phone to ring, and I would answer and hear a death threat. I got used to it. My uncle is eighty-nine this year, and he is still going strong, along with his sons, Vinicio, Juarez, and Peligrin. Vincho has had and still has a lot of friends and a whole lot of enemies. He put an ex-president in jail along with former military members who were in the drug-trafficking business. He was the drug czar during the nineties and the Clinton administration, when former general Barry McCaffery was the US drug czar. They were in many meetings together, and he earned a lot of respect internationally. I would on occasion show up in a newspaper alongside my uncle while he was making a statement. He got a kick out of it. I would be sporting these dark sunglasses, and people would say, "Vincho is working with the CIA." People at school of course knew who my family was, and it helped most of the time, but at times, if there was a professor in the opposition, it was tough. My uncle was shot at point-blank range in the abdomen with a forty-five while he was defending a case for the Dominican government in Haiti. He was left in the street to die. The then president of the DR, Juoquin Balaguer, called Papa Doc and said this: "Vincho is like a son of mine. Either you do everything possible to save him, or there will be a war like these two countries have never seen." Papa Doc's private doctors did save him, and the rest is history. Thank you, God.

By my second year, the loneliness and homesickness had not gone away, but it was more of a routine. I would still mark off my calendar and just count the days before I would go home. When I did go home, there were legendary parties. I think my parents held their breath until I was on the plane to go back. From August of 1981 to November of 1986, I would only come home twice a year, four weeks for Christmas and four weeks in the summer. I took summer school every year to catch up with my class or better my grades.

After my second year, I received a notice that I didn't meet the GPA of 2.8, and I needed to leave the school. I had a 2.7 GPA. My family did not want me leaving that school because one of the other vet schools was in La Juaz, which was a state school but very radical and basically anti-American, and the other was in San Pedro. It was full of American students and famous for problems like drugs. After a lot of letters and a meeting with the dean, my uncle came out of the office and said, "Danito, tu tienes que estudiar mas" (Danny, you need to study more). Was a favor done? Absolutely. I still talk with the secretary at my uncle's office about the letter they wrote, advocating to keep me there at that university.

At this point, with two years under my belt, I realized I had no plan B. There was no going back. I told myself, "Get your shit together, and take things more seriously." I was twenty-one years old.

I still felt alone and isolated. It was very formal down there. If you went to the movies or a club, you got dressed to the T. I never met any girls really. It was too awkward with the language. I would receive letters from some family members and a former girlfriend. She was pretty amazing, always encouraging me to hang in and not miss this opportunity. They say that girls mature faster than boys. This was the perfect example.

The gardener, Ramon, who delivered the mail, would show up with letters maybe once every six weeks. The mail took about three weeks to arrive. I would spend the day reading my letters and thinking of home.

Chapter 5

Dominican Justice, the Law of the Land

You didn't screw around with the police or drugs in the DR. I met a medical student down there from California. He was arrested for pot and spent ten days naked in a subterranean pit with boxed food once a day. He is now a very established surgeon in California. The only trouble I got into down there was a scary situation but comical. I was leaving the university and happened to get into a fender bender with my yellow Volkswagen Bug. I ended up getting into a verbal exchange, which led to a chase, where the other party was chasing me. I drove immediately to my uncle's office. The guy followed me right into the parking lot. I was in the office hiding. The secretaries were saying I had to leave and go out and deal with this guy. My family were all out at home for lunch. So I went out to meet him with one of the bodyguards, Lopez.

After some discussion, the guy convinced us to follow him to the police station to make a report. We did, and it was the biggest mistake. After some discussion I didn't really understand, Lopez said he would go back to the office and get some help. I was like, "No problem. I got this. I will fill out a report and be on my way." Soon after Lopez left, I was called to a hallway with a couple of police / military officials. They very loudly demand I take off my shirt, shoes, belt, sneakers, and socks. I was walked down a dark cement hallway and through an open iron gate into a dark, smelly cement room with about twenty guys. Some were beat up, and some were half naked. I immediately did not make eye contact and walked to a far corner. Squatting down, I was thinking, *WTF*. I was approached by one prisoner, who asked, "What the hell are you in for?" I told him about the car situation.

About an hour went by, and I could hear in the background people getting beaten up. As hour two went by, a guy approached me and said, "You know crazy things happen here at night."

The only light was from a little window with bars on it. As one guy jumped to the window and grabbed the bar, I heard a billy club on the other side hit his hand. I then heard my name called. "Daniel Castillo, Daniel Castillo."

An official came to the gate door and asked me some questions. I gave him the number of my uncle's office. He asked, "Whose number is this?"

I responded, "Vincho Castillo. I am his nephew."

In that moment, the entire cell block ran toward the guard as his jaw dropped. He said, "Who?"

I said, "Vincho, he is my uncle."

The cell block started to make fun of the guard. One said, "Ha ha, you guys just fucked yourself."

About an hour later, my cousin Juarez came and had me released. However, the next day, I had to report to another prison yard, La Preventiva, with my cousin Jose. In the confusion of it all, they locked me up again, thinking that my cousin Jose, who is an attorney, was dropping off a prisoner. I was placed in a yard with people in cages. I was petrified until I heard my name again, Daniel Castillo. An official came out to release me to my cousin and said, "You are Vincho's nephew?"

I responded, "Yes."

He was upset and said, "Why didn't you tell me? Vincho is our friend. He is one of us, and you need to tell people that if you ever have a problem."

Chapter 6

Developing a Routine

At one point, I was really homesick. I was at my cousin's house for lunch and to hang out at their pool. This was before the two-year probation mark. It was about the first eighteen months. I was talking to one of my cousins, Chu Chi Melgen. He is my cousin's cousin from their mother's side, my aunt Sogela. I said, almost crying, "Chu Chi, I am done here. My bags are packed, and I am looking into a ticket home."

He said, "Hold on. I will be right back."

In about five minutes, his mom, Tia Linda, and my aunt Sogela came out. They spent about twenty minutes with me. They were encouraging me to hang in there and get my title with my profession.

"You can do this! You will leave here with your degree and another language."

It was pretty amazing they came to me and didn't let me give up.

There were many times these brief meetings and times of encouragement would come from my family. At one time, I failed a subject, which meant I needed to make up for it in the summer. I was really down. My uncle was like "What? Una materia, one subject? No big deal. Repeat it. Take it over, and keep going."

At this point, after the two-year mark of premed courses, I was actually considering going into medical school. There was quite a bit of discussion on that from some family members in the DR. They did not realize what the veterinary profession was all about. The summer after the two years were finished, I was home in Ossining, partying and working at Stony Lodge as part of the maintenance crew, landscaping, painting, and whatever else I was told to do.

There was a picnic at the Stony Lodge Hospital pool hosted by my dad for the Dominican American Medical Association. This was where all the doctors who were from the Dominican Republic, practicing in the tristate area, would meet and basically get together and party. I brought up the fact that when I went back to the Dominican Republic in the next three weeks, I would have enough credits to enter medical school. The vet school and med school were pretty much grouped together for basic sciences in the first two years. My father and cousin Tunti, who are the only two medical doctors in the entire family, were totally against it. Then some of their colleagues jumped into the conversation. They all agreed: stay in veterinary medicine. Their warnings were all the same. "The medical profession will be taken over by insurance companies. Stay where you are."

At that point, I was all in. I had about three years to go, and I was ready to push to the next level. I was still sad leaving friends and family, but I was ready. The Dominican Republic really started to be my second home.

I think about certain episodes that stayed with me, like the one with the Black Vietnam vet and custodian at Anne M. Dorner Middle School. I was in the back of a truck working with the maintenance crew at Stony Lodge. They all happened to be Hispanic. The supervisor was Jorge, who was Cuban. He was awesome. There were two other Cubans. One was a nephew of Jorge's who came right from Cuba during the Mariel boatlift in 1979–1980. The other crew members were from San Salvador, Ecuador, and Chile. They all got a kick out of me, as my Spanish was pretty good. While in the back of the truck, I started yelling in Spanish with a Cuban accent, "Viva Fidel! Viva la Revolution! Viva el partido comunista!"

The truck pulled over, and all got out. I was approached by Jorge and the other Cubans, and they set me straight. They weren't going to harm me, but I wasn't sure. It was a serious talking to.

"Hey, Danny, you don't know what our families have gone through to get out of Cuba." The seriousness, sadness, and anger were palpable. We ended with *un abrazo* (a hug).

"Lo siento hermano," I said. (Sorry, brothers. Didn't mean any harm.)

As I entered my third year, the vet school became more intense with the work. There was absolutely no time to get homesick or feel sad. I was lonely and sad and missing people, and I always looked forward to letters from family and the girlfriend who was always positive and telling me to hang in. "This is your opportunity," she would write.

I always remember what my cousin Juarez would say as I made the decision to go to school in the DR. He said things like, "Danny, once you get in a rhythm with studying, it becomes fun or almost like a game. You get into it, and getting good grades and improving becomes fun." Juarez is my uncle Vincho's middle son. He is brilliant, just like all of them. I saw Juarez graduate college as I was entering. He was valedictorian of the entire school and of all the majors. He received sixty-four A's and two B's in five years. We are like brothers now. I am close to my entire family in the DR. He is one hell of an attorney and can convince you of anything.

We had a dinner in Boston about two years ago. Of course, the topic of politics was going strong. Juarez is a big supporter of Trump for reasons of border security. The DR has the same issues with Haiti and illegal immigration. I am more independent, as is my sister Gilda. Well, at the end of the night, we were both thinking Trump was not that bad. It must have been the mai tais at the Chinese restaurant that made us think that for even a brief moment.

I continued with my physical fitness at gyms or tae kwon do and basically studied twenty-four/seven. There were plenty of times my classmates would go out to unwind, and it all became routine. Once I really started to get into it, if I had a Saturday night off with not too much work, I would hit the clubs, and there were many in the DR. This was the early to mid-eighties, and Michael Jackson was very popular. The music, dancing, and everything else were happening. There was a casino in every hotel, which I never really got into.

I never got into playing cards or gambling. I went to Vegas once in 1994 with some veterinarians at Western States, a big vet meeting. I lost fifty bucks in thirty seconds and cashed out at the slot machines. I am just not into it. I don't buy the excuse, "Well, it's like entertainment!" I don't buy it.

The routine was Dominican style. I was completely becoming Dominicanized. I got used to having no power at night and studying with a candle and having no running water at times after spending the day on the school farm doing rectal exams on cows. Lucia would prepare a big basin for me to wash up. Eventually, the water and hot water would come, and I took full advantage. The other thing was that I had everything else done for me by my family. I lived there, my clothes were washed, and I was fed. The food that I didn't like two years earlier started to taste pretty good. I actually would look forward to it. It was and is healthy food. The main staples are rice and beans, platano (plantain), chicken, salad, fruit, and a lot of avocado. It's all so awesome. Remember the time; it was the early to mid-eighties. The nearest McDonald's was in Miami or Puerto Rico. I still craved a hot dog or a Milky Way though.

I met new people, a lot of Puerto Ricans, Cuban Americans, and a few Americans from the States. At one time, we were all hanging out, and one of the Cuban Americans just got back from the airport returning from Miami. He greeted us all with endless packages of hot dogs and buns. There must have been seven or eight of us eating hot dogs all afternoon. He would mention over and over again, "Danny, there isn't a hot dog I didn't like." It was awesome. I remember at this time understanding from another point of view real politics and how it influences others. My friend's roommate was Jose from San Salvador. He would tell us all the stories of how family members were kidnapped and killed by the death squads during a very hard time. Jose managed to escape and was studying to be a doctor. This was not the typical dorm life I would have experienced in college here in the States.

We would all get together occasionally at places to make us feel at home again. One place was the bar at the American embassy. They would open it up to us, and we would go there to hear music, play pool, hang with some of the marines, and drink Budweiser. There was another place that would have Monday night football or Sunday football. A bunch of us would go down to watch, have a few beers, and hang out. It was those things we did to feel like we were home again. One time after Monday night football, we were all about to leave when all of a sudden, they got the *Tonight Show* with Johnny Carson. The whole place erupted in applause.

I actually had the best of both worlds. I was embedded in the Dominican life and politics with my family and then would go with other groups. I was the messenger of what was happening in the country. If I heard something at my uncle's house, like perhaps there was going to be a strike or an upheaval, I would be relating it the next day to professors and classmates. Sometimes, I didn't quite understand something and would say the wrong thing. I would get to school, and people would ask, "Hey, Castillo! Que lo que esta pasando?" (What's the latest?)

I would say, "There is a strike coming," and all would be in a panic. It was pretty crazy at times. So I was basically creating rumors some of the time, and rumors would travel fast. Hey, if the nephew of Vincho Castillo said it and he has inside information, it must be true. In the Dominican, they would call it *tirando bolas* (throwing balls or rumors). Things would get pretty intense sometimes. My uncle put himself out there. He could have easily kept quiet about the corruption and drug trafficking and made a lot of money being one of the best attorneys in the country. He saw things differently, as do all of his kids and now grandchildren, who are all attorneys and following the same path. Stand up for democracy because it is fragile, and in these countries and many others, money and corruption play a big role. Once you start buying politicians and judges, the game is over. There are still good people out there trying to do the right thing. You just have to have the nerve, heart, brain, and balls to do it.

I lived through two elections in the DR, where the entire family would stay up all night surrounded by armed guards. We would wait for the vote count and hope no one had the stupidity to go against the democratic norms and overthrow the incoming or outgoing government. There were many times they would have a curfew at night where you shouldn't be out in the street. My aunts would say, "Danny, let's go to Vincho's house and see what the latest news is."

I would be driving in my yellow Volkswagen Beetle and going through roadblocks, pretty scared to say the least. Then my eighty-five-year-old aunt would start talking to the soldiers with absolutely no fear whatsoever. "We are going to Vincho's house. I am his aunt." Then they would make the roadblocks clear for our car. However, it would always end in a conversation.

The soldiers would ask my aunt, "How is your family?"

Everybody was either related or knew someone's family from way back. For my aunts and my uncle who lived through Trujillo's time, this was nothing but worth everything. Don't let a bunch of thugs try to take power and let a fragile country fall apart.

The years were going quickly, and before you knew it, I was preparing for my last year. Some of my classmates who were ahead of me were already presenting their theses, graduating, and preparing for the national boards to become licensed in the States. Many were going to Florida, because that was where they were from or Florida seemed to be easier to get licensed in. They just required the national board and another test called the Clinical Competency Test (CCT). Most other states had another practical test or were just more rigid. It seemed to be getting harder to become licensed in the States at that time.

During my last two years in the DR, things did change a bit on my trips back to Ossining. I would work at Stony Lodge more as a medical attendant. I learned a lot dealing with some of the patients who were my age or even younger. Some were doing a lot of the same BS I used to do. I started to work with the staff and occasionally go out socially with them. The craziness of all-nighters and then going right to work were gone, for the time being anyway. It was the early to mid-eighties, and cocaine was the drug of choice for many. It was available everywhere. I remember getting picked up at Kennedy Airport and then making our stop in Washington Heights with my dad. I saw an army of NYPD, having at least twenty if not thirty dealers handcuffed against the buildings. My dad's friends, who worked and lived in those areas, had a look of such sadness and disappointment watching the younger Dominican generation get caught up in it. One turned to me and said, "Danny, look what has become of some of these kids. We all worked so hard to provide a better life for our families." I will never forget it.

My grades were improving, and all was going well. Before you knew it, I was prepping for my thesis, which was on a topic of radiology. I was actually donating material for the radiology department. It was pretty awesome. For some kid who didn't speak a word of Spanish four to five years earlier, I spoke for about two to three hours presenting the thesis in front of a board. I was grilled but defended myself at this time. It was in the blood. I had five years of experience watching my uncles and cousins make statements and speeches all over. So in other words, I developed the gift of gab but now in two languages. I passed the thesis with an A and dedicated it to my entire family, both in New York and in the Dominican Republic.

It was quite a moment and achievement. I went right down to my uncle's office and announced what I had done. The party started, and believe it or not, I was starting to prepare, pack, and get things ready to return home to New York after spending from September of 1980 to November of 1986 in the Dominican Republic.

I graduated in a special ceremony in the dean's office on November 3, 1986. I was finished and needed to move on, so the general ceremony in May of 1987 would have been too long of a wait. I was a bit nervous for a couple of reasons. One reason was the unknown of passing boards and where I would end up. The other reason was when I arrived in New York, I would not be returning to my hometown of Ossining. Earlier that year, the sole owner of Stony Lodge, Dr. Luis Murillo, sold it. He gave my dad and all the other doctors and all staff about a two- to three-year notice on what was going to go down. He basically had his exit strategy in place. Many staff members, including doctors, saw the writing on the wall and were proactive. They left and landed other jobs. My dad and some others decided to take the wait-and-see approach. Well, that did not go over well at all.

It was 1985 or so, and medicine, especially in the mental health field, was changing. Drug treatment became a big business. Cocaine was bigger than ever in the eighties and really hit Ossining and the entire country. Crack was the thing. Once the new owners, who happened to be a corporation, came into town, things changed quickly. The 1-800 cocaine hotline was in play. Staff members were let go left and right. They didn't really fire my father, but they did not want him there. He knew they were all full of shit and cashing out on the patients. If you don't deal with the inside mentally and deal with those mental issues, whether anxiety, depression, or whatever it may be, you're not going to deal with the drug and alcohol abuse. I went to visit my dad in his office on my last trip to Ossining while still a student in the DR. I went to his office, where he had worked for the last twenty years. Someone asked me who I was. No one knew me. They said, "Ohhh, Dr. Castillo's office has been relocated." It was on the third floor literally out of what appeared to be a bathroom. I found him sitting there behind his desk, looking pretty ashamed and disappointed.

We had a party for my graduation in the DR on November 3 at my cousin Jose's house. It was quite a feeling. My cousin Alfred was there. He had a couple of months to go before he finished medical school. My cousin Jose was such a huge influence on me. He was there from day one, picking me up at the airport at eighteen years of age. He always picked me or my dad up. He would always say, "Danny, you will leave this country not only with your profession and degree but also another language and most importantly another culture." He drove me to the airport for my final exit. I had six years' worth of suitcases and boxes and boxes of books. As I said my farewells to all, it was very emotional. My elderly aunt knew I might never see her again. It was the end of an era. The place where I would cry nightly and be so homesick was now and is now more than ever my second home. I said goodbye to Jose with *un abrazo* (a hug). "Okay, hermano, gracias por todo" (Okay, brother, thanks for everything).

He responded, "Okay, hermano, gracias a que" (Thanks for what).

When I started vet school in 1981, my class had sixty students. Fifteen of us eventually graduated in 1986.

Our family lost Jose almost seven years ago this September. He died of a sudden heart attack. He was a great family figure, the nucleus of the family. It was and still is a major shock. I don't know if I would have made it without him. I am so grateful he got to meet my own family, my wife, Ellen, multiple times and my boys, Austin and Carter. Although they were pretty young, they do remember him. I just wish he could be involved with the accomplishments that were created in the last seven years since his passing—one of which is investing in the DR with an apartment in La Romana. How he is missed! He would have enjoyed it so much. I am very close to his wife and kids, whom I have known since they were born. They would have lunches with me almost every Sunday during my time in the DR. I am indebted to them, my family down there, and the DR as a country.

The DR is a great country with a very proud people. They are not all baseball players or drug traffickers. There are professionals, teachers, artists, musicians, and hardworking laborers. Unfortunately, the bad things make the news. I know a lot of people in law enforcement, both from SWAT, the Drug Enforcement Agency (DEA), and the FBI, and unfortunately, there is a certain population that has been notorious in the drug trade. They need to be dealt with in every sense of the word. Democracy is fragile, and it cannot be taken for granted. It is a war, and we have to continue the fight from all aspects—law enforcement, education, and treatment. As I mentioned before, in these fragile countries, where the drug traffickers influence business, judges, presidential candidates, and the military, democracy is lost.

Chapter 7

Hard Times

I graduated from the DR at the age of twenty-four. What I assumed would be a brief time living at my parents' and studying for the boards, eventually transpired into the most difficult time of my career. My youngest son asked me a couple of weeks ago, "Dad, what was the hardest decade of your career?" Without hesitation, I said, "My twenties."

My dad picked me up at Kennedy with almost six years' worth of suitcases and enough boxes of books to fill a truck. I was very unsettled as we were making our way to Staten Island. It was no longer the familiar routes of the Henry Hudson to 9A, Croton Dam Road and Grandview Ave. It was such an unusual feeling. He was describing the streets as we made our way to this new home. We pulled in, and my mom and my sister Mimi were waiting. I was speechless, in pure shock. It was a small house with a very small yard. We talked and eventually called it a night. It was the weirdest feeling, almost more so than my time first sleeping in my room at my aunt's house in the DR.

The next day, Mimi and I were having coffee in this living room. Mimi had just graduated earlier that year, 1986, in May or June. We were definitely in a bad place. Staten Island was not our home. Although my parents have been living there now for over thirty years since they moved from Ossining, I still don't consider it my home. It's where all my cousins from my mom's side were born and raised, but it wasn't ours. We were at this awkward time after college without a definite plan. I just kept telling people, "Well, after my national board exams, all will fall into place."

I would say this line to people and will continue to repeat it throughout this book: "Hi, my name is Dan. I am twenty-five. I make $3.35 an hour. I live with my parents, and I don't have a car." I was a real keeper. I decided to look in the *Staten Island Advance* for employment, preferably with a local vet. I had never actually been in a veterinarian's office in the States. I answered an ad and went for an interview. I needed to take the train to get there. Remember no car. I met the owner, Dr. Thomas Carreras, who after all these years I consider one of my important mentors. Tom was just starting the practice and worked it twenty-four/seven. My shift was 3:00 to 11:00 p.m. Tom basically worked from 7:00 a.m. to 11:00 p.m. on his own. His work ethic was unbelievable. He was tough and really was surprised by how little I knew and my unfamiliarity with how a vet practice ran. My starting salary was $3.35 an hour, minimum wage. I was fine with it. I was just doing this until May of 1987 when I would take my boards.

This short stint in Staten Island lasted until October of 1988. It was horrible. I fell flat on my face taking the boards and actually lost count of how many times I took them. The major issue was the format. It was not how I was trained; however, there were outside factors. Not to make excuses, but it was a bad time. I had trouble just getting my head in the right place. I would try to study in my room, but it just wasn't clicking.

I was also a complete fish out of water. I was Dominicanized. I was so unaware of what was happening in the States. I was also being questioned by everyone. "What? You're making $3.35 an hour, and you were in college for almost six years?"

"What do you mean you failed the boards?"

People, including some family members, would say, "You may have wasted your time in the DR." This was painful. I would visit my old girlfriend in Manhattan and was introduced to her college friends, including her future husband. They were all an awesome group and were all making the moves in the city with great jobs in finance and other exciting careers. I was so out of touch and really embarrassed that I was making so little money, cleaning cages, mopping floors, and of course living with my parents.

She asked me, "Dan, do you have a credit card?"

I responded, "No! But I will get one." So I went to the bank in Staten Island and applied for one. They gave me one with a credit limit of $300.00. I didn't have a pot to piss in. I remember being in a taxi with her and her now husband. They had a conversation about sushi that went on and on. I finally asked, "Guys, what's sushi?" I mean not long ago, I was in the DR, and the maid was plucking the chicken and preparing the rice and beans and platano. At one time, my boss, Tom, asked me to heat up his cup of coffee in the microwave. I literally had no clue what it was or how it worked. I needed to ask one of the other technicians to help.

I continued to plug away at the practice, trying to stay focused and study on my own. We would see interesting and sad cases. Crack was big at that time. I remember dealing with an owner whose boxer died suddenly because of crack being blown in his face. I would make some extra money by floating horses' teeth at a barn. Twenty-five bucks a horse. If I did five to ten on a weekend, it was extra money in cash. The problem was it was dead winter, and I didn't have winter clothes. It was the first winter after my graduation. I didn't even know how to float teeth. I was shown by the stall manager. It just looked better if a vet did it. No one needed to know I wasn't licensed. It was so cold. I had on sweats and sneakers. My feet were frozen. One of the stall workers said, "Hey, Doc, do yourself a favor, go stand in that fresh pile of horse manure."

I did. It had steam coming off of it, and it worked. I didn't give a shit. I was cold.

The boards were given in May and December. So if you failed, you needed to wait six months to retake them. I would always take them in Florida at that time. Some of my former classmates would take them with me, and we would all meet. I always needed to save money to register for the exam, the flight, the hotel, and a rental car. My credit card limit was slowly increasing to $500. Florida was the place to be, it seemed at that time, as they were just requiring the boards, which was a two-day exam for eight hours each day. The first day was all multiple choice, basic sciences, and then medicine in the afternoon. The next day was something called the clinical competency exam (CCT). It was fourteen cases, including small animal, large animal, and exotics. Very tough, but I passed that one within the first two years. The problem was you needed to take it again and again if you didn't pass the national board. As time went by, more and more former classmates decided to bag it. The process was becoming too complicated and expensive. Some classmates had children and families and literally needed to put food on the table. A group of classmates seemed to pass a lot quicker than I did for a couple of reasons. One, I believe, was maturity. They all at least did their undergrad in the States and had a much better background than I did. The other reason was attending a course in New York City at the Animal Medical Center (AMC). The AMC is known worldwide. It's a phenomenal facility located on York Avenue in Manhattan. They offered a six-month course of complete immersion for the foreign graduates like myself. It was twenty-four/seven of cases working with the top veterinarians and learning the American way. They actually included a large animal section at the Bolton Center at the University of Pennsylvania at the vet school. Unfortunately, it wasn't in my plan. It cost about five thousand dollars at the time. I had zero money, and my parents wouldn't offer. A friend of my dad's tried to get me a loan, but what bank was going to loan to someone making $3.35 an hour, which was about four thousand dollars a year? It was upsetting and still is, thinking about it, but then maybe I wouldn't be where I am today with all the people I met and family I have. What I did instead was get the notes from the course, including the tape recordings. It reminded me of being in the DR when I would tape all my classes with a little tape recorder and listen to it all night. At least this time, it was in English. It definitely helped with the notes and the recordings but not enough to get me over the edge in passing the boards. Things were getting very frustrating. I was now twenty-five and approaching twenty-six, and I really wasn't getting anywhere. I was hearing it from friends and even family. "Why aren't you passing the test? Was that school not good enough? How about trying something else?"

Trying something else was not an option.

By May of 1988, I passed the boards for the state of Florida. Everyone was asking, "So when are you going to Florida?" I was hesitant. I knew people in Florida, but I wasn't eager to go. My boss, Tom, was a bit taken aback. "Danny, why don't you go to Florida and start working as a veterinarian instead of staying here as a tech for [at that time] five dollars an hour?" I felt if I went to Florida, it might restrict me from going anywhere else, and I was right. When laws were changing with licensure and foreign grads, I found I had made the right move.

I also had a job offer at the Staten Island Zoo. I was called by a Dr. Vince Gatullo. He heard about me and offered twenty-five thousand a year and time to study to take my boards. He couldn't believe I was declining it. I had multiple phone conversations with him, and he was really taken aback. The Staten Island Zoo is a very well-known zoo, especially for reptiles. I felt I should do, and I was right, just what some family members told me in the DR: stay focused on your end goal. If you get too comfortable in a position or with money, you will take your eye off your goals—something similar to not going back for undergrad in the States and then returning to the United States. I don't regret not doing that at all. At that time in my life, I was not ready for the college scene. I wasn't mature enough, and it could have been a disaster. I felt if I took the job at the zoo, I would have gotten real comfortable with the money and neglected my end goal. Who cares if I am not licensed? At least I have a decent job. Yeah, right!

The summer of 1988 was about the lowest I could go. I was getting more and more frustrated. I had a friend from Ossining, Chris, who was living in Staten Island. He had a very good position at UPS. He worked it out for me to get an interview and drive a truck in Canarsi Brooklyn. I left Tom's practice. It was just getting more and more frustrating. Tom, I believe, was a bit frustrated with me. He was supportive, but even he would say, "Dan, you are not getting anywhere, still living at home." It was hard. I don't think people mean to hurt others by what they say, but believe me, they do, and everyone had an opinion. My goal was to make some money that summer in UPS and then make a move to Florida, but I was still unsure about the whole idea.

I started at UPS with a three-day training session in Queens. Driving on the BQE (Brooklyn Queens Expressway) with an old Plymouth Volare car with no AC and a hole in the floor was horrible. I hated every minute of it, and it was the lowest of the low. Nothing against UPS, but it was not in my cards. People could tell right off the bat that this was not my thing. I was not a trucker. I had surgeon's hands, very smooth and well manicured.

The summer of 1988 was the hottest summer in one hundred years. It was brutal. I would drive to Canarsi, dreading the gathering of all the truckers. I was first put in with supervisors to learn the routes and how to be as efficient as possible. I did learn some things, for instance keeping my keys in my hands as I approached my car. UPS did a study on how much time you waste looking for your keys in your pockets. I was also told I could urinate in a bottle in the truck to save time. That was not going to happen, as it was too busy and loud in the back of a truck. I needed quiet areas, so I would stop off at a McDonald's or something to urinate.

The worst was backing the trucks in side by side, inches apart. There was no way I could do it. Guys would make comments or crack on me. I absolutely hated it. At the end of the day, I would have to go into a room where all the truckers would count up their money for the COD deliveries. This was in 1988, and nothing was automated yet. It was horrible. I would be sweating; steam would be coming off of everyone's head. This was when the uniform was pants only and black Knapp shoes, no sneakers. The room literally seemed to be divided, Blacks on one side and Whites on the other. They all talked and got along, but it was definitely noticeable. The White guys were not too friendly when it came to helping me. I had this look about me that I would most likely go into management. The Black group was much more willing to help and show me something if I wasn't sure.

One morning, I didn't know what route I was going to get. A couple of the Black guys were talking about Brownsville and Bed Stuy, where Mike Tyson grew up. I was definitely nervous and asked, "You don't think I am going there today?" with fear in my face.

They all burst out in laugher. "No, my man, they ain't sending you there. Chill out."

I was so relieved.

The respect that I gained for all these truckers and that company was amazing. It is a hard job; it was the hardest I ever worked. You needed to run and deliver, and you were getting timed along the way. Efficiency was everything. I never understood the routes and always got lost. I was with my supervisor one day after about six weeks into it. He was timing me and coaching me from the truck. I was so hot and frustrated I threw the boxes up in the air. My supervisor, Tommy, who was a friend of Chris's, was like, "Dan, what the fuck are you doing?"

I said, "Tommy, I have to talk to you."

"What's wrong?" he said with concern as he was watching me almost in tears with frustration.

I said, "Tommy, I am a fucking veterinarian!"

"What?" he said. "A veterinarian?"

I confessed that this was a short-term deal for me to make extra money. He was so cool and felt so bad. He said, "Dan, you got to get the fuck out of here. Maybe you will treat my dog one day. Keep working hard. You will get there."

I spoke to my friend Chris on a Zoom meeting a couple of months ago. I asked about Tommy. I guess he has a very good position in that company and is doing great.

I left at the end of the day after counting up my money and said goodbye to Tommy and no one else. I just walked and never looked back. I ended up going back to Staten Island to 62 Virginia Avenue, where my aunt Sissy's house was. I did that every day after the UPS job and met with my uncle Mike, my cousin John Burke, and my cousin Anthony. They would look at me beet red, hot as hell, and shake their heads. There was a pool in the backyard, so I would always take a dip. They all kept telling me to hang in; it would all fall into place. My uncle Mike and cousin John have passed on. They are missed and were both there in those difficult times. Like my cousin Jose in the DR, they weren't there with opinions. They were just there to talk, laugh, and support.

CHAPTER 8

Fate from a Phone Call

In late August, early September of 1988, I was home going through the motions of studying for the December board and planning an exit to Florida, but again, I was doing it half-heartedly. The phone rang, and I answered. It was my friend Bill, who was from Worcester, Massachusetts. He graduated in the DR with me but about two years earlier. He had heard and knew firsthand of the struggles getting licensed. He mentioned he had a position for me at the University of Massachusetts Medical Center in Worcester. They were in need of a veterinarian for research surgery, and you did not need to be licensed. He didn't need to convince me to come up and interview. They were offering fifteen thousand a year with full benefits. What was also very entertaining was Bill was practicing at a vet clinic, and Tufts University School of Veterinary Medicine was twenty minutes away. He mentioned that they had meetings there along with the Massachusetts Veterinary Medical Association (MVMA). It would be a great environment and a new start. I flew up for the interview, which was just a formality really. Bill highly recommended me. Bill and his wife, Deb, picked me up at the Worcester Airport directly from Newark. It was a great time and weekend. We went to see the new sights, and the hospital was amazing with at that time five thousand employees and a huge library for all the medical students, which I was able to use. I got the job and was on my way in two weeks.

I left Staten Island and my parents' house with about three hundred bucks in my pocket, a credit card with five hundred dollars in credit, and the same piece-of-shit Volare with a hole in the floor. I think about that difficult time in Staten Island. I do realize things happen for a reason, whatever that may be. In my case, I think if I were to have remained in Ossining during those difficult years, I might have gone down the wrong road again with some old friends. The frustration was high, and the failures were many. Thank God during those two years in Staten

Island living at my parents' making $3.35 an hour, I at least had my sister Mimi around. She was starting her own journey. She graduated Cortland with a major in Spanish. She substituted in the New York City school system, which was very hard. Through her own hard work and perseverance, she obtained her master's in social work at New York University and has her own successes.

Bill and Deb were willing to put me up in the back room of their triple-decker house off of Brosnahan Square. It was close to Holy Cross, and it was definitely a college town and environment; however, I was now already twenty-six years of age. The first day I showed up to work, the manager of the research project at that time was a human surgeon named Nilima Patwardan. She called me into her office, apologizing. She said, "Dan, you are three weeks too early. Perhaps you can get a job at Burger King for the time being."

I just went with it. I was nervous with no money, but I was happy I was there. I responded, "No problem. I will come to work with Bill at no pay and continue studying for the boards." She was so impressed and happy to have me. It turned out after I officially started work, the human resources person paid me ten hours a week in overtime to compensate me. It was pretty awesome, and the environment was excellent.

We were doing pancreatectomies out of greyhounds and then eventually pigs. The only issue was they were nonsurvival surgeries. However, you needed to be on your mark. There was always a team from the research company who was funding the entire grant standing over you. The animal needed to stay alive throughout the entire surgery while the team waited and cultivated the organ in a cooler. They eventually brought it to their headquarters. We then started to implant the insulin pump into the animals and monitor blood glucose around the clock throughout the night and then surgeries in the morning. It was pretty amazing, and the animals started to go longer and longer. That was where I came in, surgeries in the morning, monitoring overnight, studying when I could seven days a week. I met great people at the hospital, and I am friends to this day with some.

Welcome to Massachusetts. We don't like New Yorkers. That's what my impression was and still is in some ways. Massachusetts is my adopted state. I obviously made a good living and life here. It is my home. However, they will detect your New York accent in a second and then start questioning. It's all pretty ridiculous, but it's a fact. Boston is great, but it's a town, nothing compared to New York, much less New York City. The bars in New York will close at 4:00 or 5:00 a.m. In Massachusetts, it was maybe 2:00 a.m. You couldn't even buy alcohol on Sundays. These were important things when I first arrived in Massachusetts. Now I really don't care what time the bars close because I'm in bed by 9:30 p.m. anyway.

About a good month into my living conditions with Bill and Deb, there was a sudden change. I came home one night, and Deb asked to speak with me. Her words were like this. "Danny, I am going to ask you to leave for a little while or come back later. I am divorcing Bill tonight."

"Okay, say what?"

I came home later, and nothing was said to me, so I went into my room and made believe nothing was happening. The next day, it all came out. Bill was devastated. Deb was having an affair with his best friend. All I wanted to do was get somewhat of a normal life. I arranged another living deal with a mutual friend Lisa. Lisa was willing to put me up in her extra room of another triple-decker apartment. Bill was really upset because he was planning for me to pay some of the rent money. It was just not going to work, so I went with Lisa. I still saw Bill at work, which was awkward.

The living conditions with Lisa were very interesting to say the least. My first week there, I came home on a Sunday late afternoon, about 5:00 or 6:00 p.m. I had been at the hospital all day working on the research project, monitoring the dogs and trying to study at the same time. I was starving, so I stopped by DiAngelo's, a sub shop, to pick up dinner. I climbed the triple-decker totally exhausted. As I was about to take my first bite into my steak and cheese, there was a very firm knock at the door—a persistent, firm knock with someone demanding I come out. It was a female police officer demanding I step out to be questioned for a hit and run. She started to question everything, who I was, where had been all day. You would think by the scrubs that I was still wearing she might have backed off a bit. I was told to follow her down to the street, as there was a young couple standing by my piece-of-crap Plymouth Volare. The questions continued with a more accusatory fashion. "Where were you? You are from New Yaaak" with that bullshit Boston accent.

I started to plead, "I was at work all day." They were accusing me of hitting the couple's car down the street because it was dented with yellow paint and my car was yellow.

After about thirty minutes, and I don't know why I didn't think of this earlier, I said, "You can please call my supervisor. He was with me all day." I was literally begging and very nervous and afraid. I really couldn't believe it. She started to question the New York plates that I still had and the condition of the car. She pronounced my last name and in a way was questioning where exactly I was from. For a minute, I almost said I was guilty. I was thinking maybe I did do it. This was a complete shit show. Suddenly, the boyfriend or husband turned and said, "Are you sure this is the car and guy?"

She turned and said, "Well, maybe not."

I was relieved, but there was absolutely no apology or anything. It was like "Okay, have a good night."

The police officer said nothing either.

About a month after this episode, Lisa started dating a shady character. I could tell right off the start that this was not going to end well. He had all the prison-like tattoos and was very rough around the edges. He was also unemployed. Both Lisa and I would come home from work, and this guy would be hanging in the apartment drinking beers. One night, after getting back late from work and trying to study in my room, I heard the beginning of the two of them arguing. The argument got louder and louder as I sat there thinking what my next move was. A memory crossed my mind of an episode in Ossining when I was sitting at a bar in the Crotonville section. I was hanging with an old friend Matt, who had played lacrosse with me in high school. A biker gang walked in, and they were all standing behind us while one of the members and his girlfriend sat right next to us. All was cool, until a brief argument between the two of them started, and he managed to grab her by the hair and slam her head against the bar. Matt looked at me without hesitation and said, "Do not make a move or say a thing." We went about having our drinks, and within minutes, the biker gang all left. So I was sitting in my room, and now I could hear the fight escalating. It started to become physical. I was used to fight or flight from growing up in Ossining. So I proceeded to jump out my window in my room that led to the triple-decker staircase to my car. I immediately drove to Bill's house, and we called 911. Within minutes, the cops came and locked the guy up. Remember back then there were no cell phones. It was quite an experience. Lisa was mortified and tried to tell me all was okay, but I knew I needed to go, which I did in the next month.

Things were also about to change for the better. In reality, it became a life-changing opportunity and chance that would guide me to where I am now. While working at UMass, I decided to call Tufts University, located in Grafton, Massachusetts. I basically wanted to see if there were any volunteer positions or anything I could do just to see the place. I was connected to a Mrs. Card, an elderly woman who coordinated the volunteer program. She listened to my story and suggested I speak with a Dr. Bob Murtaugh. I hadn't heard of Bob at the time, but within a short time, I realized who he was. I will never forget what he did for me. We are still friends and keep in touch.

Chapter 9

Hard Work Pays Off

Bob Murtaugh at that time was running the small animal hospital at Tufts. He ran the intensive care unit (ICU) and was a brilliant guy. He was double boarded in critical care and cardiology. We spoke on the phone, which was very intimidating. He had a very deep, monotone voice. He was open to meet with me later that week. I was so nervous to go. After I got out of work, I put on a suit and my winter overcoat. This was January or February of 1989. I found my way to the campus and presented myself to the reception desk. His name was paged, and within a few minutes, as I asked the receptionist a question, he tapped me on the shoulder. In that monotone voice, he presented himself.

"Hi, I am Bob."

I said, "You're Dr. Murtaugh?"

He was a bit shorter than I had expected and was wearing Levi's, cowboy boots, and a tight Def Leppard T-shirt. He was also sporting a Mohawk-type haircut. He asked that I follow him to his office as he gave me a quick tour through the hospital, introducing me. It was absolutely awesome. The staff, doctors, residents, and technicians were all so nice and all introduced themselves by their first names, never using the term *doctor*, which was hard for me to digest. We went up to his office, which was decorated in Minnesota Twins souvenirs. He sat behind his desk with his cowboy boots on top of the desk and basically talked for at least an hour. First, we talked about the Yankees and New York. He then started to listen to my story. He listened more and asked a question or two. I made him laugh with some of the topics, but he just seemed to absorb it all. He ended with this: "I don't know, Dan, but I do know this: you are going to persevere. Welcome on board. You're more than welcome to help in the ICU."

I did so after I got out of work at night and overnights. I was completely thrilled and so grateful.

I continued working at UMass for the next month, volunteering overnights, and trying to study. At times, I would come home, and Lisa would watch me cooking something up in the kitchen. She would laugh watching me literally fall asleep at the stove. I found another apartment just for me with no roommates. I found it through the university, through one of the staff members on the project. It was pretty nice. He was a nice guy, although he didn't let me use his washer and dryer, which he said that I would be able to do. It was too late, and I couldn't make another move. I was pissed though, as I had to fight with everyone at the Laundromat. I also started to realize I needed to build up more credit and develop a checkbook. Most of my living was below the grid or under the radar. I was twenty-six/twenty-seven, and I had never even balanced a checkbook. The brother of a very good friend of mine from Ossining lived in Groveland, Massachusetts, up north about an hour. He was an accountant. I made it a point to visit him every time my bank statement came in through the mail. He would sit down with me and would help me balance a checkbook, and I mastered it. It is amazing how many things I did with no money. If I went to visit New York to see friends or family, I would have a hundred bucks in my pocket. It is pretty crazy thinking back. How the hell did I do it?

In March of 1989, I went to work at UMass, and we were all called in to Dr. Patwarden's office. We were told the grant had been withdrawn, and now we were all unemployed. This was six months after I had moved to Massachusetts, and now I was unemployed. I was devastated and was a bit unsettled to say the least. However, I was under control. There was this part of me that came out of almost a survival mode. No time for BS, I needed money and a job and had no savings. I called Bob to let him know that I might not be there to volunteer for a while as my grant was pulled and now I was unemployed.

Without hesitation, he said, "Hang in, Dan. Let me talk to a couple of techs. We may have an opening here as a technician. There is a Dr. Mary Labato who wants a technician to help her at night. You can do this and study for your boards. It would be a great opportunity." I was and am to this day grateful for what they did for me. I started there the next week, and what I thought would be a short stint ended up being a three-year deal. It was the experience of a lifetime.

I started my first day, which was an introduction to all my fellow technicians who all happened to be female. It was a very interesting time. For the most part, people were trying to figure me out. Is he a technician? But a vet? Is he from the Dominican Republic or New York? I basically did my part to work my ass off. It was definitely overwhelming with the care and knowledge all around. To be honest, some of the techs didn't want me involved, specifically my supervisor. They thought I was filling the time until I got my license, and then I would be out of there. They were right, for the most part.

One hurdle after the other was thrown in front of me relating to the boards. I first met Dr. Mary Labato, who was a specialist in internal medicine and urinary/

renal disease. I was nervous when I met her with, "Hello, Dr. Labato. I am Dan Castillo."

She responded with a quick, "First things first, you call me Mary."

I was her shadow in and out of exam rooms. Then I would take the patients to the wards and follow all of her orders. She was always guiding me and helping me think like a clinician. I wasn't just performing the technical skills; my brain was being picked by other clinicians and residents. My shift was 12:00 p.m. to 8:00 p.m. This allowed me to participate in small animal rounds with all the other students who were on the internal medicine rotation. Small animal rounds were at 4:00 p.m., which was perfect, right in the middle of my shift. You would hear staff members like Frank Pipers alert everyone on the loudspeakers to report to small animal rounds. It was awesome and intimidating at the same time. I was able to sit, listen, and basically watch all the students get grilled by the residents and other clinicians. You needed to be prepared and know your shit. Most students were very prepared and very bright. Most students did their undergrad at very good colleges, like Yale and Harvard, very top-level universities. I became friends with many and all of the staff and residents. The residents also would enter the wards and ask me to give care to their patients while they moved on to others. They were always grilling me for my thoughts on what was happening medically and what my plan would be. This definitely rubbed some people the wrong way. I would later find out it rubbed some professors—not many but a few—the wrong way as well. For the most part, all were very supportive. This was in 1989 to 1992, and people like Peter Kintzer, Mike Stone, Ed Maher, and Ginny Renko were all in the game. They have all gone on to do some amazing moves in the profession. Pete Kintzer and I hit it off right away. He was from Brooklyn, another bright guy who was just as comfortable talking about Wrestlemania as Cushing's disease or any other medical topic. He would become a major player in my future.

My goal was to pass the boards with a high enough grade and eventually practice in Massachusetts. My contacts with New York were dwindling, and my life was seeming to be more settled in Massachusetts. At times, I would get together with the students and study for the exams. This was the time I remember specifically how inept or inferior I felt. It was a very tough feeling. They would seem to get into a rhythm, answering board questions with absolute ease. I continued to struggle. The board would be given in downtown Boston. So I would drive the night before and spend the night at my sister's house. She was living on Clarendon Street. I remember driving in December with no heat in the car and a hole in the floor, absolutely freezing, spending the night, and walking the next day to the exam, completely nervous and unprepared for some reason. I would catch up with the students I studied with, and they were all taking it in stride. So I kept moving forward. I would have sit-downs with Bob Murtaugh or Peter Kintzer and Mary Labato, and they were all on the same page. Keep fighting; you will persevere.

My trips to hook up with some old friends from Ossining were very rare, maybe two to three times per year. When I did go to visit, it was with a sense of "Well, I deserve to binge for the whole weekend; I am working hard." I was definitely feeling more distant from that crew as my circumstances were completely changing. The last time I did go down was in October of 1989. It was for the Rolling Stones' Steel Wheels tour at Shea Stadium. It was basically a three-day party. When I returned to my apartment in Worcester, there were fifteen messages on my answering machine. Everyone was trying to locate me to inform me my dad was in the hospital in the DR. He had had a heart attack and would be there for a couple of weeks to get stabilized before returning to New York for a full workup. I felt terrible and went to work on that Monday looking like I got shot out of a wind tunnel.

While I was treating a dog in the wards, a resident approached me and said, "Dan, you are not looking too good. I don't know what you're up to, but don't blow your opportunity." I was about to break down and told her about my dad. It was all good, and it was my last time partying at that extreme level, a pure waste of time and very risky. On a good note, my dad had a quintuple bypass at New York University that December. He was sixty-one years of age at the time and will turn ninety-two this August. I just went down to see my parents last weekend, as I haven't seen them in three months because of COVID-19. Hanging out, having pizza and beer with my dad at ninety-two and my mom at eighty-five is not a bad deal.

One day, while working in the wards, I met a student who was different from most. Sydell Katz was older than all. She was in her mid-fifties and was a senior veterinary student. She would see me working my ass off and talk to me. She listened to my story. She was a former teacher, I believe, and got into vet school as a second career. She was the mom of four children and married to her husband, Brian. They were from New York, like me, and we seemed to hit it off pretty quickly. After hearing my story one afternoon and about my struggle with the boards, she, in her New York accent, said something to this effect: "Hey, Danny, don't ever be intimidated by these kids," meaning students and some residents. "They were trained to take that exam from day one of vet school. Their entire format seemed to be a prep for that exam." She asked what my work schedule was and offered for me to go to her house and study for the next round that December of 1991. We studied, and she explained to me the whole thinking process two days a week for at least a couple of months.

At this time, I was dating my now wife, Ellen, who was a technician in the ICU. We knew and had worked with each other or at least saw each other at work on a regular basis. I dated some other techs as well, but Ellen and I seemed to be more friends until we both agreed we would go out in May of 1991. The joke is that she stalked me all those years, and I would decline her advances, because I was above that. After our first date, which was at the Piccadilly Pub in Westborough, we have never been apart. Although we each had our own apartment, we were always together. It was a settling situation and also guided me to settle down and eventually stay in the area. We planned a trip to Florida in December of that year after another round of board exams. I started really studying like a true maniac. Sydell had graduated, and I was using all of her techniques and advice. Sydell and Brian would talk to me with all this confidence of what my capabilities were. She would see me at work and say, "Danny, you got it going on. You're personable and knowledgeable."

Sydell and Brian were planning to start a vet practice in Chesapeake, Virginia. She would describe the place, and it sounded beautiful. She was also willing to take me on, hire me, and eventually allow me to become a partner, which was what my long-term goal was. So when she graduated and left, I was sad actually, but she was always in touch via a card or call, encouraging me to work hard and get ready to move to Virginia.

It was Labor Day of 1990, and my future brother- and sister-in-law had a party. I went up with Ellen, and something really came over me. It was like, *Enough bullshit, I need to pass this freaking thing and get on with my life. If this girl is even going to stay with me, it has to happen.* For some reason, Ellen and I were left to watch Brian and Pamela's home the next day after the party. I had all my materials with me and said, "This is it." I started studying again at their house and continued every single day for hours in my apartment while Ellen did things around the apartment and waited for me. I would be in my room for hours. Our only social life was a movie on the weekend or going for a motorcycle ride for a couple of days. I had bought a motorcycle from Bob Murtaugh the year before. I eventually sold it after two summers and never looked back. Don't miss it at all. The studying went on for the next three months. I had index cards throughout my entire apartment, and I completely devoured the *Merck Manual* and made notes of every page.

Chapter 10

One Roadblock after Another

Exam time came, and a day or two after that, Ellen and I took off to Florida. We went to Orlando, Miami, and Fort Myers and flew out of Tampa. We watched the Giants and Bills in January 1991 with an old friend of ours at his home. It was a great trip, but all along, like so many times before and for so many years, it was in the back of my mind. I knew that when we returned, the letter would be there waiting for me. I was on edge and really didn't know what to think.

When we returned to the apartment, the letter was there waiting to be opened. I opened it with such anxiety and saw the results: "Congratulations *you passed*." It was one of the proudest moments for all, including the staff at Tufts, Ellen and her family, and my family. It was one big relief, and no one would be able to take it away from me. It was one big party as well, as I would make some brief trips back to New York on occasion. The party was short-lived; the journey needed to continue. It was far from over. The rules for foreign grads were changing, and I needed to do one of two things. One option was to go back to school as an intern for a year, unpaid—actually, I needed to pay the university. The schools at that time were mostly in the Midwest and South. They were offering this year for the foreign grads. This was not an option for me. I didn't have the time or money to pay tuition, and there was no way in hell I was moving to the Midwest or down South. Option 2 was something more entertaining. It was the CPE, the clinical proficiency exam. This was an exam given in Starkville, Mississippi. It was a five-day, eight-hour-a-day exam that was completely hands-on, practical. The cost of the exam was two thousand dollars. I missed the registration for the May exam, because I did not yet have the grade from the national board exam. So I eventually registered for the September 1991 exam. It was a bit of a wait, but I had no other choice, and I was in the best work environment that anyone could be in prepping for an exam like the CPE.

Sydell and Brian were also elated, as they had started construction on their new clinic and were saying the fall of that year was perfect timing. I would take and pass the CPE and eventually go work for them. It was an opportunity I couldn't pass up. I also got a promotion at Tufts by running their research facility on campus at the Peabody Pavilion. It was awesome. Some of the staff, mostly surgeons, would have a project, and I would set up all the surgeries and anesthesia. I could also go back up to the hospital and get prepared for my exam. It was a perfect combination. Plus, it was more money. I was making twenty-seven thousand, so all was good. Peter Kintzer, whom I knew as a resident but who relocated to Georgia for another title of some sort, returned to Massachusetts and was now my supervisor. It was not a bad deal, and I had no other option. The only thing that was holding me back was that I didn't have the two thousand dollars to register. I felt guilty asking my parents, and they actually never offered throughout the journey. Remember the AMC course? So I was pretty frustrated but needed to game my name on this list for the exam before I got bumped and was waitlisted. Out of the blue one night, I got a call from my aunt Sissy. Her words were like this: "Danny, you have come too far to let this hold you back," and in forty-eight hours, she sent me a check for two thousand dollars. I registered, and I was off.

Life was good. I continued to work in my new position with Peter Kintzer as my direct supervisor and Glen Spaulding, who was coordinating all the projects at the Peabody Pavilion. It was a different position organizing surgical research projects for staff members at the hospital. We eventually started to work with human surgeons from Boston. They would arrive in groups of twenty or thirty to practice new surgical instruments on pigs that we would set up under anesthesia. It was quite an experience listening to the surgeons ask the medical reps how to work something new like a laparoscope. I would actually hear them say things like, "Okay, I have to remove a gallbladder on Monday. How do I work this contraption?"

I spent many days a week driving four-hundred-pound sows from Tufts Vet School in Grafton to Massachusetts General Hospital in Boston. The pigs were first choice to learn and practice on for the human side. After hours, I would go into the hospital and absorb as much as I could to prepare for the CPE, which would be in September. I actually flew down to Virginia with Ellen to visit Sydell and Brian and see their new clinic being built. It was called Chesapeake Animal Clinic and was a storefront next to a Sherwin Williams Paint Store, on Battlefield Boulevard. The area was beautiful, and we were taken to see all the sights. Virginia Beach was twenty minutes away, the city of Norfolk fifteen minutes away, and the Outer Banks a little over an hour. Sydell and Brian were building a beautiful home on its own pond in Duck, North Carolina, next to Corolla.

Chapter 11

Just Keep Going

As I was getting closer to the date of the exam, I was becoming a bit more anxious. This was a very, very tough exam. It was divided into sections, all practical. You had to perform surgery whether it was a canine spay, cystotomy, or splenectomy: anesthesia, clinical path, radiology, emergency medicine, and then large animal—horses, cows, pigs—the entire gamut. I started to get all my flight and hotel reservations prepared. It would take three flights to get to Starkville, Mississippi. Then I arranged a ride to the hotel from one of the other students. Most students were from Ross University down in St. Kitts.

The test was a complete shit show. It was the most strenuous, high-intensity, degrading thing I had ever really been through, and that says a lot, knowing my history. It was eight hours a day, and I was completely grilled by the residents of the school who were giving the test. I did feel very comfortable and at ease in surgery and all of the small animal parts. There was one time while doing a spay when I had a resident standing on the other side of the surgical table, barking out questions, which I answered one after the other. He then asked me to throw some hand ties or knots. I can do them blindfolded and worked at UMass with human surgeons. I did it humbly and with ease, but inside I was like, "Go fuck yourself." The large animal part was a different story. I struggled. They had sections of paperwork as if you needed to transport cattle from Texas to Louisiana and do health inspections. I had to break down and put together surgical instruments like a fetotome for a fetotomy as if a cow were having trouble delivering her calf. I had to treat horses with nerve blocks and do a lameness exam. It was tough, and the stress was killing me. I needed to run from one section to another.

The hardest thing I dealt with was understanding their southern accents. It was a horrible experience. At night, I would gather in the hotel with the other students and talk about the test. I was exhausted, and at night, after all that I had been through, I had the most difficult time sleeping. It felt like I didn't sleep for a week. At the end of the week, we all went our separate ways, and there was no love lost with anything about the students, teachers, or the entire university.

Everyone at Tufts was interested in how it went. I just could not tell, and grades would not be in for another six to eight weeks. So I just had to wait it out. Sydell asked that I visit again and see the finished practice. This was in November of 1991. I spent a couple of days with Sydell, Brian, Ian (their youngest), and one of the older daughters. They had four children. It was a great time, and we were really gearing up for me to move down there and join. Things were pretty serious with Ellen, and it seemed like they were more interested in that as well. The last night I was at their place, after we all went out and had dinner, the phone rang. It was Ellen. She felt the need to tell me at the time, as awkward as it was, that I had failed the test. I believe she wanted me to know because I think I told her I needed to know ASAP so Brian and Sydell could prepare. It was devastating news, and it felt like all the air went out of everyone's balloon. However, it was like fight or flight kicked in again, not just from me but the entire Katz family. It was sad, but what were my next options? I needed to finish this out, and I was so close to doing so. The flight home was long, and when I returned, I strategized with Ellen my only option. Getting waitlisted to repeat this exam and wait another year and pay another two thousand dollars was not an option.

The only option I had besides waiting another year for the CPE exam was to complete a year internship or senior year at a veterinary school that was providing this program for foreign graduates. Tufts just so happened to be providing this program to two candidates that year. As I mentioned, most of the schools that were offering this program were in the Midwest and South. This was basically another year of school in clinics, in both small and large animal medicine and surgery. It was unpaid, and actually you had to pay the year of tuition. This was when I believe I went into a serious fight-or-flight mode—actually just fight mode. I connected with Bob Murtaugh, Peter Kintzer, and other clinicians at the hospital.

Bob Murtaugh was the main one who stepped up to bat for me to see what Tufts could do, if anything, as far as having me enter the program. It was weeks before I heard any feedback. Finally, I was told that the academic board was going to have a meeting with regard to my situation. This was all done before social media and scanning and email correspondence. Imagine me calling down to the DR and asking to have my transcripts mailed. The procedures took forever, and it was exhausting. It was multiple phone calls to the American Veterinary Medical Association (AVMA), letters of recommendation, and a never-ending process. Finally, the board convened. While I was working, I was absolutely on edge.

I went up to the hospital during break to see some coworkers. I heard that the board finished the meeting. While I was in the hall, one of the board members who was on the academic committee saw me and said, "If it was up to me, I wouldn't even consider you in the program with your grades, let alone this building."

Now this was a professor whom I saw on a daily basis while working in the wards at the hospital. My heart was in my mouth, and I just responded, "My vet school wasn't in my first language," and that was all I could say. I was devastated and sad, but then the Ossining, New York, side came over me, and I said to myself, "Go fuck yourself." I told Bob, Pete, and some other clinicians what had happened, and they said the same thing: "Tell him to go F himself."

I was then called to the head office of the chair of this new committee for foreign grads. He was a nice guy, a surgeon but an academic, a paper pusher. Anyway, he basically proposed this: "Dan, we have an option for you. We decided we are going to put you through our own test. You will be tested by our staff over the next couple of weeks. After I get feedback from our clinicians, we will have another meeting."

I said fine. I knew the staff, as I had been working there, but they did grill me and question my thinking and my skills. After a couple of weeks, the following was decided. With the time of my employment and the testing, they accepted me into the program. Instead of doing the full year, I only had to do six months. They felt I had tested as high as any other student, and I had been there for three years. It was a very good deal, and I was thrilled. The only problem was when I was sent to the finance office, I was told that the tuition for the six months was eighteen thousand. I went along with everything they said, including signing documents to start in two weeks. I was definitely feeling the pressure, wondering where the hell I was going to get eighteen thousand. It started to bug me, and as I mentioned it to some of the clinicians, like Bob, they were all like, "Oh my god, are you kidding?"

Chapter 12

Fight Mode

I was in my office one morning about to get started for the day, and my supervisor/friend Pete Kintzer walked in. He knew my dilemma of having no money and also knew I was starting to get nervous. I was agreeing with everything Tufts was offering except I had no freaking money. Pete mentioned I should give this guy at Iowa State a call. Dr. Ronald Greer was the head of the foreign grad program. I called at lunch, and it was this refreshing Midwestern voice that was willing to help.

"Hey, Dan! Dr. Greer here. I hear you have a problem, and I think we can help. We'd love to have you come join our program for six months. Can you start next Monday?"

I was elated!

"Is there a way you can do a month of overnights in ICU?"

I was yessing everything he said. I asked, "What is the tuition more or less?"

He responded, "Four thousand, but don't worry; you can pay that when you get to Iowa." He also proceeded to give me a number to a hotel down the street that was giving interns like me a room at four hundred dollars a month. It was down the street from the vet school. When I hung up, I turned to Pete and said, "Hey, Pete, how the fuck do I get to Iowa?"

Pete had done his undergrad at Iowa State and responded, "Cross the George Washington Bridge, drive for two days, and make a right at Des Moines." He said, "Dan, go and don't look back. Take your shit, pack your trunk, and go. You don't have to say anything or explain anything to anybody, specifically Tufts."

I went to Bob Murtaugh and explained. He was very happy and also recommended that I go and go fast, no need to say anything. I also wanted to make sure all would be certified. I already had the six-month certification at Tufts, but it was always in the back of my mind that something might go wrong.

I discussed the plan with Ellen and her family, as well as Sydell and all involved. The program was to start at the end of March 1992 and finish August 1992. I was then planning to go to Virginia in September. That being said, it would be nine months away from Ellen. So to make it official, we got engaged. It's a bit crazy to get engaged and then leave for nine months, but there was no way I would have her moving around, following me until I was at least employed. Ellen was right there for me, packing and getting ready, as we were also keeping it from all at work. I felt if the administration found out I had taken the offer at Iowa, they might take back the six months they offered, plus they were expecting my eighteen thousand in tuition. Some of the clinicians, like Bob, were providing me with contacts, other professors, at Iowa. The veterinary field is small, and many are connected in one way or another. At this point, there was one other problem. I didn't have the four thousand for the tuition in Iowa. So I drove to Staten Island to say goodbye to my parents and also to meet my cousin Tunti. I basically told him the situation. He pulled out his checkbook and wrote a check for four thousand. I also had a deal with Sydell and Brian. They gave me a loan for four thousand to be paid in increments while I was living in Iowa. It was for food, rent, and other living expenses.

Ellen and I packed my car, which by then was a 1980 Fleetwood Brougham Cadillac. I had bought it from my friend's brother from Ossining. He was the brother who taught me how to balance a checkbook. Well, this car belonged to their other brother, who at that time was doing time in jail. It's a long story that I would rather not get into.

We hit the road over the George Washington Bridge and onto Route 80. As a matter of fact, we had our AAA TripTik maps out. This was way before GPS. We stopped in Cleveland for the night and then proceeded for another eleven hours on day 2. It was actually a nice ride, very easy and nice people all along the way. I had a check for the tuition, the four hundred for the hotel room, and a couple hundred in my pocket.

While I was driving, my mind would wander, thinking, *How will I compete at the school? I can't believe we are engaged*, or *I can't believe I will be gone and won't be with Ellen until our wedding*, which was to be in December of 1992. Ellen's sister was married in October of that year, and her cousin Kenna was married in August. I managed to make it to both of their weddings.

As we pulled in and drove around the university, I thought it was quite impressive. We made it to the hotel and were greeted by the staff. Everyone—and I mean *everyone*—was willing to help. The hotel room had a minifridge, a microwave, a sink in the bathroom, and an extra sink in the hallway, used to wash dishes. There was no stove. We made the place look presentable and comfortable. We took a ride to the school and met Dr. Greer and some of the staff. All were unbelievably nice and welcoming. We spent the next two days settling in until it was time to take Ellen to the airport to go back to Massachusetts. This was where I completely lost it. I had been on overdrive for so long, and it all came to a freaking halt of reality. *What? She is leaving? I won't be with her until December?* It was a hyperventilating cry and an awful drive to the airport. It was tough but all part of the journey.

I also had this feeling at this stage of my life I was still unsettled, moving from place to place, jumping hurdles and having to prove myself. I was going to be thirty in the next two weeks. As Ellen returned to work at Tufts, I guess she was approached by many board members asking where I was, as I was supposed to show up with my eighteen thousand. I left and didn't turn back, but I owe so much to the entire staff at Tufts University. It was my savior in so many ways.

Iowa and Iowa State were awesome. No other words to describe it. The people and the school were all so supportive. I never really knew what it was like to have people stop you to say hi and really be in no rush at all. It was truly a genuine feeling I had from everyone. I was always nervous about going to rounds and being grilled by the professors and clinicians. I was in for a totally different experience. It was more of a confidence-building session. The clinicians seemed to want to build the confidence of the students and assure them that they knew their material and this was what they would see in the real world. Both schools were great, but each had its own way. I have discussed this with some Tufts colleagues, and the first thing that comes into the discussion is the caseload at Tufts. It has one of the highest caseloads nationally, and you need to move. Iowa was a much slower pace. I did my first month there in ICU on the overnights, and it wasn't what I expected. At Tufts, there was no way you had time to put your head down. The cases were incoming all night. At Iowa, it was every once in a while. So I really did what I could do and helped out wherever possible. It was confusing for a lot of staff members. They could see I was more advanced than any of their senior students, and I also had this New York accent. People would ask, "Wait. You're a foreign grad? What?"

I moved on to large animal farm work with one of the ambulatory doctors, visiting all the local farms with cows, pigs, and sheep and whatever else came our way. It was an amazing experience. The farmer families would greet us with food and gifts. Their children would be there as well. I would ask, "Why aren't these kids in school?" The reply was that they would get a better education out there on the farm. Some kids would have a finger or two missing because of accidents with farming equipment or any other hazards of the farm life.

I remember watching the sky turn a greenish color off in the distance. I asked, "What is going on?"

"Oh, well, Dan, it's tornado season, so we will try to avoid that area."

Okaayy.

The living at the hotel was not bad. I made the best out of it. I was in the best shape ever for a couple of reasons. One was I was at the school working twenty-four/seven. The other was I had no stove. My lunch on a daily basis was canned tuna out of the can and yogurt. I was 186 pounds. That is pretty lean for a guy who is six feet two inches. I was also a member of the gym down the street from the hotel. They gave all the students in the hotel a deal we couldn't refuse. I always found time to work out and play tennis with a new friend from Denmark, Claus Helsted. He was a student as well and was going to be finishing in the next three to four months. Claus and I have been sending Christmas cards since 1992. I saw him at a meeting in 1994 in Vegas, but we always kept in touch. He was fascinated with the American life, cowboys, and the western part of the country. He has been living in California since he left Iowa and has a very successful practice. His girlfriend, Benda, would come and visit from Denmark, and Ellen would come from Massachusetts. We would all go out to see the scenes of Ames, Iowa. It was a good time. It never got easy having to drop Ellen off at the airport. We managed, but it was always very difficult. I celebrated my thirtieth birthday on a huge cow farm. Some of the students, all female, along with the professor and the owners of the farm, got me a cake. It was and is an amazing part of our country.

The rotations at the school were all going well. I did realize then that this entire program, called the exam commission for foreign veterinary graduates (ECFVG), was a good thing and needed—not for me of course, but I had so many other experiences and was lucky to have it. At Iowa, there were some students from the Mideast, South Korea, and South America. I will be honest. It looked like some of them had never seen an IV catheter before. So the other students and clinicians came to me for any workups or treatments of cases.

I remember I had one weekend off. It was the first one in many months. We would work weekends all day and night. Claus happened to be off as well. It was a great night. The restaurant downstairs in the hotel was a Mexican place. It had great margaritas, Coronas, and nachos all night. Then we had Sunday off, so we would go to the big shopping market down the street called Save U More. They would have large meals, big barbecues and steaks. It was the one day of the week I could afford to eat and catch up on the yogurts and tuna from the week before.

I reported to morning rounds on Monday morning and was approached by a resident, Dr. Davis. He was pissed and pulled me aside. "Where were you this weekend, Dan?"

I said, "I was in my hotel at home."

He informed me that I was on call and had left everyone hanging.

I responded, "Please, Dr. Davis, I didn't see my name on the list. I am sure of it."

Then he said, "Let's see what Dr. Greer says about this and you finishing your program here."

I was shocked, floored, and so upset I was speechless. I also had my New York attitude, which I managed to keep inside. "Don't fuck with me now." I marched right into Dr. Greer's office.

They all could tell I was upset. They told me not to pay attention to Dr. Davis and also assured me I was doing a great job and they were happy to have me. I almost started to cry with so many mixed emotions. The other residents from large animal also assured me that the schedule that weekend was a complete shit show and disorganized. I also learned and did realize before this episode that some people are always trying to throw a roadblock in your way or play head games or are just plain mean. It turned out that this Dr. Davis is an excellent vet, and last I heard, he has been doing a lot of work for animal welfare both nationally and internationally. He once reached out to me about a project in the DR for animal welfare that I have been involved with since 1994.

The clinics and daily farm calls, as well as my mental and physical relief at the gym, all became a way of life. Ellen came out to visit a couple of times to see the highlights of Ames. We once took a ride to a man-made lake. We packed a cooler and spent the day. It was not close to New England or the Adirondacks, but it made do. I made the best I could of one of the lowest budgets I have ever had. I was paying four hundred a month for the hotel, and Brian and Sydell sent two hundred a month. They were so nice to front me a loan of $4,000 while I was in Iowa with the plan I would repay at $333.00 month once I started my job with them the day after Labor Day.

I always get the question "What was the most unusual animal you ever dealt with?" Without hesitation, I mention an experience in Iowa. We were in rounds in the large barn/hospital during clinics. We would visit from stall to stall, reviewing all the cases with a diagnosis and treatment plan. We approached a stall with an emu, an Australian bird. The resident and clinician running rounds handed me and two other interns a large stomach tube and asked that we pass it to relieve a possible gas or other obstruction. The three of us were trying to corner this massive animal. All of us were getting thrown around like rag dolls. The bird had these massive claws with talons, which literally ripped my pair of Levi's from groin to ankle. We eventually did it with a lot of work. I almost felt we were asked to do this as somewhat of a head game. It was quite a day.

I remember one farm called me and another intern to castrate 125 pigs. We would just pick them up by the hind legs, upside down, spray them with betadine, slice, slice, rip out, and rip out.

At one point, one of the doctors who happened to be new was staring at me. We had this feeling that we both knew each other. He finally asked, "Do I know you?"

I was a little hesitant, but I asked, "Were you one of the professors giving the exam for foreign graduates at Mississippi State?"

He smiled and said, "That's right!" He remembered me taking the test almost eight to nine months prior. I asked him, "Do you think these American students would pass a test like that?"

He shook his head and said, "No! That test was made to fail people!"

I shook my head. "Well, that is the reason I am here in Iowa."

As time went on, a new class of students entered, and all of my so-called friends moved on. I especially became somewhat friendly to a group of students from the Mideast. I would actually have lunch with them, and all were very nice and worked very hard. One student from India named Canwall would say things like, "Dan, you don't seem to be like all of the other American students." He mentioned that I was the one who went out and introduced myself and was friendly. He also mentioned I was one of the only ones who talked to my family on a weekly basis. On Sundays now for four decades, I have given them updates. Most times, I talk to them two to three days in a week.

As I was reaching the end of my Iowa chapter, I was getting a lot of praise, thank-yous, and good lucks from all. Claus left a month or two before I did, and that was tough. One memory that stands out is my family had a wedding shower for Ellen. So Leanne, my sister-in-law, and Ellen drove to Staten Island, and the shower was held at my aunt Mary's house. Aunt Mary became the matriarch of the family after my grandmother passed away.

I had just gotten off a farm and was cleaning up in my hotel room when the phone rang. I heard the sound of a houseful of people singing "O Danny Boy" on the other end of the phone. I felt so far away but so close at the same time. I remember being on a mission to pack my car and all my belongings from the last six months in Iowa. The plan was to have Ellen fly to Des Moines the day before, and then we would both take the two-day trip back to the East Coast. People thought she was crazy, but that was what we planned.

That night, I received a call from Ellen, who was very upset. The weather from Boston all the way into Chicago was very bad, and it was still tornado season. She was delayed in Boston for many hours and might or might not get to O'Hare airport. The plan we concocted was I would leave Iowa at 2:00 a.m. and meet her at O'Hare by 8:00 a.m. the next day. After I got directions from the staff at the hotel, my plan was in place. I would pack the car and just drive straight for eight hours. This was before cell phones and GPS. I did it and found my way to the airport in traffic. Sitting curbside was Ellen. She had just exited the airport five minutes prior. We hopped into the 1980 Cadillac and continued eastbound. Youngstown, Ohio, was our first stop to sleep. We stayed in a little motel. The kitchen was serving all game-animal-type food—bear, alligator, and deer. We made it to Massachusetts, and there was another party.

We attended Kenna and Joe's wedding and then made the trip to New York to see my parents. It again was all happy but unsettled and sad because I had about a week to get ready and start my life as a full-time licensed veterinarian. This was 1992, and I graduated in 1986. So six years after I graduated, I was licensed in three states: Massachusetts, Virginia, and Florida. The time was fun but short-lived. I packed up the car again and was soon Virginia bound. I didn't even discuss a salary with Sydell until this point arrived. I felt so indebted to them for lending me money for Iowa and Sydell's support on passing the boards.

I remember her asking me how much was I making at Tufts. I said, "Twenty-seven thousand."

Her response was "Okay, we will pay you $27,500.00."

I was very naïve and just went with it and agreed. There were no other discussions of benefits like health insurance or vacation. I just went all in. I was going to rent another room from a girl who was right next door to Sydell and Brian's. She was in the navy and was going to be away most of the time. It was hard leaving again, no doubt, but the goal and the promise was to stick with the plan and move forward.

Chapter 13

Virginia—Great Experience but Tragic Times

"Virginia is for lovers!" That is what their motto says. I will remember it for pure tragedy and sadness, and it was where I went through some of the best clinical work that helped build my broad foundation.

I arrived in Chesapeake, Virginia, on Monday, Labor Day, 1992. I arrived at Sydell's condo, where she and her son greeted me with a very warm welcome and hugs. Ian, her eighteen-year-old son, was ecstatic talking with me about my new chapter. Ian was supposed to enter Florida State that semester but couldn't because of a car accident he had had three to four months earlier. He was delivering pizza at his job and was in a very bad car accident that left him in a coma for three weeks. Through hard work and with his family's love, he pulled through. He seemed perfectly fine that night and was most excited about voting in his first election that November. He also needed to settle for a community college until he was completely recovered from his accident. He was left with some minor delays from what I could see, maybe in speech or in his coordination. However, he was as sharp as a tack and was very engaging and personable.

I showed up to work before start time, which had been my ethic since vet school. Sydell and I went through the cases and had some minor surgeries to do before noon that morning. The plan was to break at noon. I went to walk across the street to open up a checking account with two hundred dollars. Remember, I hadn't been working in the last six months. Sydell went to pick Ian up to take him to register for community college. I returned in fifteen minutes to the brand-new clinic, and the receptionist, whom I had just met that morning, said, "Dr. Castillo, there has been a very bad accident. Ian shot himself. Sydell arrived home to pick him up and found him."

My jaw dropped in shock. The other two staff members were a licensed technician named Donna and a nineteen-year-old assistant named Christina. They were both in tears and in shock. The phone rang, and the receptionist said it was Brian, Ian's dad, calling from New York as he had just gotten the news. He asked to speak with me. In a very commanding voice but obviously upset, he said, "Danny, I will be down later tonight. I need your help. I can't have my wife go back into that house. Please go down and clean whatever you can clean out of there and just get back to the clinic and take care of the appointments in the afternoon."

I went into automatic pilot and said, "Whatever you need, Brian," but my heart was in my mouth. I turned to the staff and told them what Brian had asked me to do. Christina, the nineteen-year-old, immediately offered to help, while the other two were in complete shock. I drove to the condo where I was living, which was next door. I found the hidden key and walked in with Christina. We were both in shock and nervous. We walked through the entire place and came to the master bedroom, where we saw a large bloodstain about three feet in diameter on the white bedroom carpet. We walked out and went downstairs. I thought for a couple of minutes and then took a steak knife out of the kitchen cabinet. I proceeded to go upstairs with Christina. We cut out the area of the rug with the knife and placed it in a trash bag.

Within an hour, I was seeing appointments. Some news was getting out, but we didn't want to announce anything. Some clients decided to return. Some clients were like, "Okay! My cat is constipated."

I didn't realize until later that day that I had Ian's blood on my shirt and tie. I believe Ian was buried in Florida next to his grandparent. I am not sure, but he was buried within twenty-four hours as is done in the Jewish faith.

I went to my new apartment and called Ellen at work at Tufts. The entire school was informed, and the news spread. Some were advising me to return ASAP and get home. My loyalty was with the Katz family. They were the ones who provided for me during Iowa, and Sydell was really a major influence who helped me pass the boards. There was no way I was going to leave this family in this time of need.

I didn't see Sydell for a couple of days and just continued to work the clinic the best I could. Although I was very well prepared in theory, I had really never seen clients, treated their pets, and done surgeries all at once. It was definitely overwhelming. The first night after the tragedy, I was in my apartment making calls to Ellen, friends, and other family members. There was a knock at the door. I answered, and it was a very nice woman in her thirties with a very nice southern accent. She introduced herself as Pat. She was a licensed vet tech and assured me there would be people, other vets from her practice and surrounding practices, who would come and help me or who were just a phone call away. It was an amazing support group that developed very rapidly. If I had to do surgery on a dog with a mass the size of a basketball, a local vet would come help. Pat was awesome, and the friendship developed. Ellen arrived in December after we were married, and we all became very good friends. She eventually married a mutual friend named Bill, who was a Norfolk detective. The four of us all became very, very close.

About two days after the incident, I was at the clinic working when Sydell, Brian, and the entire family came, including the grandparents. It was such a sad, tragic situation, as some tried to go about business as usual. The emptiness and sadness was palpable in everyone. I met Ian's older brother, Todd, who was my age and recently married, I believe. He was an attorney in Mobile, Alabama. As the family left to take flights to Florida, where Ian would be buried, I continued to plow through the practice and do the best I could. I started to meet clients who then became friends as well. It is something to say in this profession. It has provided me with lifelong friendships.

Within a week or so, Sydell was at the practice. Her husband, Brian, continued to travel to and from New York. He would arrive on Thursday in Virginia and return to New York on Sunday nights. That basically left Sydell and me together a lot, as Ellen was still in Massachusetts, and we were also living right next door to each other. Brian was a chiropractor and was in business to start practices and then sell them. His plan was to do the same with the veterinary industry. At least, that was what I was told. The entire plan for me being down there was eventually to become the owner or part owner of the practice. They treated me as their surrogate son. We did everything together. We ate out, went food shopping, everything. We took a couple of trips to their house that was being built in Duck, North Carolina. It was beautiful, and the plan there was to get a license in North Carolina as well and work there on weekends. Within four to six weeks, things started to turn, and I became very stressed.

Sydell was going into a major depression. She would be talking and in midsentence completely break down and cry. She was distraught. I would be in an exam room with a client and hear her howling in her office. I tried to talk to her, but what could I really say? I am a parent of two boys now, and looking back, I see that what this poor woman had to deal with was too much. She would say things to me, like she didn't want to live anymore. If we were crossing the street, she would say, "Danny, I hope I get hit by this car."

I tried to tell Brian, but it seemed like his answer was just to keep her busy to take her mind off of things. I was their distraction and someone to lean on. We did everything together, as I was not married to Ellen yet and was living right next door to them. I remember going to the movies quite a bit. We went to see *A Few Good Men*. It was a great movie. There was a scene where a marine dresses in full uniform as he prepares to testify. He pulls out his gun and shoots himself. It was a very tough time, as I was sitting between Brian and Sydell. I was holding Sydell's hand. She was completely distraught, crying uncontrollably.

As my wedding was getting near in December, Sydell and Brian got the invite, but Brian had to decline. It would have been too painful for them to attend.

I managed to get my own apartment in November and move in with my bed that I had had since Worcester, Massachusetts. It was a nice place, big, two bedrooms, two baths, large patio, and a pool, all for about $550 a month. I was meeting more and more clients who knew my story and knew I was waiting to get married. They all wanted to meet Ellen. One family that stands out in my mind was that of a guy named Michael Rystrom. He and his wife had one or two very young children. He was a navy pilot. Ellen met him briefly at a Blockbuster video rental store. He was giving me a hard time, saying, "Hey, Doc, you have been married only a month and you are already staying in and renting videos?" They had a very nice-looking Alaskan malamute.

Literally less than three weeks later, I heard that Mike's plane had gone down in the Black Sea. It was a horrible time, and I remember seeing this young wife coming in with the dog and her dad after this tragedy. My respect for the military and their families is deep. When you see these families and their sacrifices firsthand, it takes things to another level. I cannot pinpoint the names of another family, but they were awesome. They had two cocker spaniels. The husband was the captain of the USS *Wasp*. They really liked me, as I would take the time to know them and spend time with them. I eventually got a tour of the ship, and it seemed like almost every sailor was a client of mine.

"Hey, Doc! How you doing?"

It was pretty awesome, as Sydell and Brian were with me, and they could see in a short time that I already had a following. There are these little things that they taught me that I still do to this day. They go a long way. I would carry a clipboard with all the clients that I saw that day and call them the next day or so to check on things. I still write welcome cards and get well cards to everyone, as do my associates here in Franklin. This is what I do. No matter how busy you are, you need to acknowledge the clients. This was drilled into me, and it's what we do at my practice almost twenty-eight years later.

Our wedding was beautiful and a great time. So many friends and family came from New York. We had a lot of the Tufts crew there as well. I remember all were intrigued with my situation and how the hell I was handling it. It was also bittersweet, knowing that the next week, we would be packing up Ellen's apartment and a U-Haul and heading down South. It was hard. No one in Ellen's family had ever been away. They are a tight group who all moved to Framingham from Prince Edward Island. It was a huge jolt to the family. As they all pitched in to load up the truck, we said our goodbyes, and it was tough. We both slept at my in-laws' the last night, and the next morning, as we headed out, it was really tough on her parents. We headed down the highway with a large U-Haul and her piece-of-crap white Renault trailered behind. She had never been in Virginia until we arrived later that night. I had to make a couple of detours. I didn't realize

I couldn't drive commercial trucks on the Palisades Parkway. I had to turn around and head over the George Washington Bridge.

The next morning, after nine months of being engaged from afar, we found ourselves in a different state. I was already used to it after three months, but for Ellen, it was very different.

That morning, Sydell and Brian came and greeted us with hugs and cheer. They asked us to look into the closet where the washing machine would go. I was saving up for one and planned to buy it that week. There was a brand-new washer and dryer with a red ribbon on it. It was so nice and thoughtful. I had to warn Ellen about Sydell's emotional breakdowns in public.

The first time it happened, Ellen was disturbed and heartbroken. Now that we were married, I spent less time with Sydell, and there was a guilty feeling as well. She was left alone, while Brian was away Monday, Tuesday, and Wednesday. The stress was building up because of Sydell's spiraling. It was by far not getting better but worsening. The staff was stressed. They were young kids, and I was really a rookie, hungry for some real guidance professionally. Sydell was a great person but no surgeon, and because of her issues, her thought process was erratic. It became very tough, and I felt divisions were apparent with Ellen.

There was a visit from their older son, Todd. He saw the writing on the wall and knew this might not work out. He was very supportive of me and was admitting that this situation was too much for anyone. I needed to think more about my wife and our own needs as a married couple. Todd was just an awesome individual.

By February or March of that year, two to three months after our wedding, there was a local vet offering me a position. I was not interested, although it was tempting. I was loyal to this family. At that time, word may have gotten out. I believe this was the time Brian wanted me to sign a contract. I just knew I couldn't commit, so I tried to avoid the discussion. It was some formula with a base salary and quarterly bonuses but had nothing about ownership. I was much more interested in mentorship and wanted to be in a larger practice with multiple vets.

There were so many nights that I would toss and turn and wonder, *How can I keep doing this?* Ellen landed a very nice job as a vet tech with Dr. Peter Fisher at Pet Care Animal Hospital. She was doing great, and that was the type of place I wanted to be at. She was so supportive of me through this entire ordeal. I kept avoiding the discussion of the contract until one day at lunch, Sydell mentioned to me that I needed to sign the contract. With a heavy heart, I just shook my head no and said, "I can't sign this, Sydell."

As I walked out, she said, "Danny, if you won't sign this, you can't work here."

She said this with a shaky, broken voice as my back was turned and I walked out. It was a devastating feeling, but I was relieved as well. I got home and told Ellen, who was also relieved. However, I had only been married for three months

Barking Big 69

and walked out of my job with nothing lined up. This was a bit overwhelming, to say the least.

One of our friends was in between jobs and was in the process of writing up his résumé. He said he could help update mine as well, and we went to the copy/print store and printed out one hundred copies. Within three days, I hit the road. I would dress as if I were going to work with my shirt, tie, and shoes. No sneakers. I decided to hand deliver every résumé in the Virginia Beach, Chesapeake, and Norfolk area. There was a part of me thinking with the last name Castillo and my initial education in Santo Domingo, I wanted them to see me in person. Within one week, I was getting calls from multiple vet practices. I was officially a relief veterinarian. I had the experience and definitely the personality to do that line of work. I would go with the flow. I took the staff members' lead from the receptionist to the technicians. I wasn't demanding and didn't throw my weight around. I was working full-time at this and making a lot more than $27,500.00.

At this point, my father and mother-in-law were making a trip to visit as they were on their way to Florida. I was at one of the clinics doing relief work, and one of the staff members asked me to come to the phone, as there was a Dr. Sydell Katz who wanted to speak with me. It was very stern in some ways, not a call to ask how I was doing for sure. She just wanted to remind me that I still owed her about $2,000. I paid the $2,000 out of the six months I was working for her, paying $333.33 a month. I responded, "No problem. I plan to pay you back."

As my in-laws were leaving after the trip, my father-in-law asked me how much I still owed the Katz family. I was telling them about the phone call from Sydell the day before. He gave me a check for $2,000 and said, "It is best you pay them off, call it a clean slate, and move on."

The next day, while at work, I wrote a note to Sydell and Brian, saying, "Thank you for the opportunity, but this will end all personal and professional relationships between us." It was sad but also very relieving. They hired another vet within a couple of weeks, and I was offered a full-time position at a phenomenal practice, Acredale Animal Hospital. Dr. Andy Gordon called me at our apartment and hired me without even seeing me. He was good friends with Ellen's boss, Peter Fisher, and I was very well known at Peter's practice. I actually did relief there as well. I asked Andy, "Wait a minute. You want to hire me full-time? Not relief?"

His response was "Yes, Dan. Come down and meet me. I heard about you. I have a full-time position with all the benefits at thirty-five thousand a year."

Ellen and I were relieved. We had just gotten to Virginia and decided we needed to give it at least a year. At the end of it all, we gave Virginia three years total.

Acredale Animal Hospital was an awesome place to be. I went over to meet Andy Gordon; his wife, Stacy; and their partner, Robby Evans. It was a very big and clean practice with at least thirty employees. It was one of the state-of-the-art practices with boarding and grooming. It had protocols like a dress code. It was very professional and most of all offered mentorship. I started on Monday 8:00 a.m. to 12:00 p.m. Then we would start back up at 2:00 p.m. until 8:00 p.m. They knew, as did many, of my situation and the tragedy with the Katz family.

At about 5:00 p.m. my first night at work, one of the receptionists asked that I take a phone call. It was a local colleague who was also friendly with Sydell. She asked if I was sitting and said that she had some terrible news. She basically told me that Sydell had shot herself at the practice, and the staff was asking for me.

My new boss, Robby, noticed the shock in my eyes and asked if I was okay. I said, "Robby, you're not going to believe this," and told him what happened. He asked that I just take a breather in the treatment room and then come to talk to him. He said, "Dan, you have been through a lot, and now you have a great opportunity and have a good thing going. Whatever you need, just let us know, but you need to know you have all our support."

Andy came in the next morning and was just floored. It was such a tragic situation that I just so happened to be involved with. I did go over after work that night and meet with some of the staff members. They were obviously shaken. They let me in and showed me where it occurred—in her office. All the evidence was still there; it was a horrible sight. They asked where was I working and said they would send clients to me if that was okay. I was just in total shock.

I fit right in at Acredale. It was a fast-paced practice, and I learned so much. We would do C-sections on bulldogs almost weekly. Andy was very connected with the breeders and did a lot of artificial insemination. I did a lot of surgeries as well. The first orthopedic procedure I did was on a duck. They gave me the freedom, and I went with it. It was amazing. After about two weeks, we had that duck swimming around in the tub. The practice strived to do all the right things with staff and protocol. They at one point had members of vet economics down to do an appraisal and give their input. The practice was rated very high in growth and protocol. Ellen and I felt more at home, but it was always on our mind to move back to the northeast. We were closer and closer to friends like Pat and Bill but always seemed to be heading back to Boston or New York. At that time, you could take a plane for a hundred dollars round-trip direct from Norfolk to Boston on Delta.

After my first year at Acredale, I was given a raise to $42,500 a year, and things were going well. There was another thing that I learned while at Acredale. The practice was state of the art with computers throughout the entire building. I didn't even know how to type at that point, and I was about thirty-two years old. I enrolled in a night class to learn how to type and passed with a high grade. I was the oldest one in the class, and the teacher really liked my effort. It was a very proud moment. The last and only typing class I had was in middle school, and I did not take it seriously at all.

We were living the life of a married couple with no kids, working, going to the beach, and having visitors. Some crazy cases would come in, but the most memorable were the cases of parvovirus. I learned quickly to manage, treat, and save these patients from this deadly virus. I remember almost being mauled by a pit bull at the satellite clinic, Rosemont Vet Clinic. If the dog hadn't been tied up on a hitch at the front desk, I would have been dead.

I was offered a contract by Acredale but refused it because our goal was to relocate back to Massachusetts. Acredale didn't want us to go, but I knew it was the right thing, and I shouldn't sign if our intentions were to leave. I took a trip up to Massachusetts to do some interviews to feel out the water and possibly make a plan to relocate. I rented a car for a long weekend and headed up myself, as Ellen had to work. I was on a mission to get back but wasn't too sure what was out there. I had some interviews lined up, specifically one that was almost offering a position over the phone. I stayed at my in-laws' house in Framingham. It was a little weird not being there with Ellen.

The next morning, I called the first practice that sounded promising, and they informed me that the position was filled. This is typical of some veterinarians; they have no clue and no manners or ethics. It just so happens that this practice is about fifteen minutes from me now. My in-laws felt so bad for me; they were crushed actually, as was I, but I had no time to BS. I said, "Okay, no problem. I will be back tonight for dinner, and I will see what is out there."

Gene, my father-in-law, showed me how to get to the Mass Pike and slipped me a hundred bucks. I initially refused but eventually took it, as I was in need of it. On the first day, I interviewed from Danvers, Massachusetts, north of Boston, through some practices in Everett, Walpole, and into the Cape. I drove for almost ten hours, three hundred miles or more. Some of the offers were asking that I start the next day, and they said that I needed to buy a house because apartment complexes were not like they were in Virginia.

The next day was the same, and I got an offer from a practice in Walpole. I verbally took it but needed to have Ellen come up for another trip and check out the area. We were both overwhelmed with the prospect of moving back and not having money to do so, certainly not having enough to buy a house. It is funny when people say, "Why don't you buy something?" and in the back of your mind, you are thinking, *Yeah right, I don't have a pot to piss in*. I had this gut feeling that the timing was not right to relocate to Massachusetts. I was sitting in the office of the satellite practice and called Andy at the main hospital. I came right out and asked, "Andy, is there any way I can take a second look at the contract?" He was elated, and we signed on for another year at $42,500.

Within six months, Vet Economics came in, and they decided to change the pay structure, which was awesome. It was a base salary with production, and my salary increased to $48,000. The issue was the following year, we were all making too much money. That was the bottom line. This was where things got sticky, and things were said that weren't meant to be said.

Andy and I have talked about it and laughed, but at the time, it was what made me leave. I was informed that we were going back to the salary pay with no production. The problem was the salary was less than that of the prior year with production. I tried to talk to Andy and explain, "It's less than with production."

At one point, he said something like, "I can get two vets for what I am paying you."

My heart sank, and I felt really upset. It was an insult and set the tone to buy me time to make a move. I started to look around, and at this point, Ellen and I said, "This is enough with Virginia. We will eventually make a move." I went to a couple of practices and spoke with the owner of a practice in the middle of Norfolk. She was running the practice for her husband, who had passed away a couple of years before. On the spot, she offered me $55,000, with all the benefits. I wasn't happy with the practice but knew in six months we were done.

When I went to see Andy and tell him I wasn't going to sign the contract, all hell broke loose. There was a lot of yelling between Andy, Stacy, and Robby. The staff was upset, but I walked and started the next day in the new position. Ellen and I had dinner with Stacy and Andy in Boston years ago when their daughter was going to Boston University. We talked and laughed about this, and now I see his son just had a baby. They are truly a great couple and ran a great practice. They helped me and Ellen through a very difficult time. We have kept in touch. They actually sold the practice and moved south. They are a huge part of my incredible journey.

I started my new job in downtown Norfolk, Virginia, at a very large practice. It was all business, and I really didn't like it at all. I knew we would be moving in six months, so I decided I would put up with policies I did not agree with at all. The owner would post the production of all the vets on a monthly basis. I don't know if it was to create a competition, but it was ridiculous. Because it was in downtown Norfolk in not the best area, I do remember leaving at 8:00 p.m. after my shift and sprinting to the car. Gangs were all over, and I just didn't feel safe. On more than one occasion, I would be working a Saturday, and some gang members would bust through the door with a shredded-up pit bull, place him on the reception floor, and run away. Dog fighting in that area was pretty common, and it was horrible to see these dogs torn to shreds. I would do what I could to help and relieve the suffering, but eventually they would be euthanized.

I remember the O.J. case was in full bloom at that time. I was home for the verdict when he was declared innocent, and I remember feeling sick inside, thinking they just let this guy off after killing two people. As I arrived into work, I saw the neighborhood and a lot of the staff were elated. It was at that time I realized how divided our societies are. Looking back and getting into detail of that trial, the only thing the dream team of attorneys had to do was to create doubt. They sure did when you heard things come out of the mouth of the main detective, Mark Furman. When you look at the history of the police and the Black community in Los Angeles, it didn't take much at all to create doubt.

Ellen and I took a long weekend up to Massachusetts as I went on an interview with a feline spay and neuter clinic in the south shore town of South Dartmouth. I accepted the offer. It was $55,000 a year with all the benefits. This was to be a temporary job just to get us established back in the northeast. Ellen was able to get her job back at Tufts in the anesthesia department. I took the job under the condition if I spayed and neutered all the cases that day, I could leave and do relief work somewhere as a clinician. They agreed. As our time in Virginia was ending, we were going through the closing of our apartment with leases and found a condo in Norton, Massachusetts. Norton was a central location. It was about forty-five minutes for me to get to the south shore and forty-five minutes for Ellen to arrive in Grafton. I was shell shocked regarding the rent of $950 a month not including utilities.

This time, I coordinated with the Beckons moving company, and it was amazing. This was the time before GPS, and they were able to calculate that we would all meet in two days in Norton, Massachusetts, at 11:00 a.m. They were right on target. It was amazing. The days of loading trucks and moving were over.

As we were leaving Virginia, we were going through the stresses of last-minute tasks. I remember this story that I still tell regarding the customer and the place of business. I had to drop my car off at the mechanic; it was a Mercury Grand Marquis. I was in a rush and stressing. When I called, the nice receptionist in her southern accent informed me that the car was not ready yet. I went off, demanding and saying some things that were out of line and hung up.

Three minutes later, the phone rang, and it was the owner. In a very nice, calm southern accent, he said, "Dr. Castillo, we would like for you to take your car out of here. We are really nice people and don't deserve to be treated like that."

I had my tail between my legs and begged them to fix the car to get ready for a long road trip. I apologized and felt horrible. I use that method with clients now, but sometimes, I use a much, much harsher version.

The last night, we spent with Pat and Bill. It was very hard and emotional. Those two were our anchor in Virginia. We were all very tight. We always wrote cards back and forth and kept in touch but never got back to Virginia, as life was getting busier.

In March of 2011, I was working here at the clinic in Franklin, and one of the receptionists asked that I get to the phone because there was a Dr. Brian Kim on the line from Virginia. Brian was one of our friends that we all hung around with in Virginia, but I hadn't heard from him since we left in 1995. He said, "Dan, I have some very sad news! Pat and Bill ... it appears it's a murder-suicide."

My heart sank, and I just felt like all the air went out of me. I had to go home and tell Ellen, which was very tough. There was no rhyme or reason to it, and no one has the answers. Bill was a detective in Norfolk, and I am sure from what he had told me, he saw some pretty tough things. Maybe, it was PTSD, stress—I just can't explain it. I mentioned Virginia is full of tragedies. There are multiple reasons why we haven't been back. Some great things happened in Virginia, but at the same time, some very sad and tragic things happened to people in my inner circle. I never attempted to reconnect to the Katz family. I just wouldn't know what to say or how anyone would react. It was all so painful. I actually attempted to look them up on Facebook but without success. I do pray for that family and do love them for what they did for me. It is just a very sad situation and one of many events that make you cherish every day and realize how life can change in a New York minute.

Chapter 14

Going Back to Massachusetts

By the time we arrived in Norton, Massachusetts, and relocated, I was already connected with veterinarians throughout the state. I had been a member of the MVMA for many years and would receive the monthly newsletter. I would read all the job openings and maintained a close relationship through Tufts.

In 1994, while I was still practicing at Acredale, I read an article from the then president of the MVMA, Dr. Bob Labdon, who was the owner of Veterinary Associates of Cape Cod. He was describing a spay and neuter program he spearheaded with Dr. Jay Meriam and Dr. Rich Roger, whom I knew personally and who helped me quite a bit as I was preparing for that dreadful CPE exam in Mississippi. The spay and neuter program was being held overseas, of all places in Samana, Dominican Republic. I was totally shocked, as this was the place that I and my entire family had known for centuries. I called Bob immediately and introduced myself. I was determined to register for the next trip.

That year, Ellen and I connected a flight from Norfolk, Virginia, to Kennedy and were off to meet people we had never met before in our lives. There was a part of me that felt I was returning home. I met Bob and the Boston crew at the gate. It wasn't hard to identify them, as they were all sporting Boston Red Sox caps. We hit it off immediately. They all really got a taste of my situation in the DR and were taken aback. I had a chauffeur and an armed guard.

When we would all meet for lunch after a busy morning of work, I would meet the crew with the chauffeur and bodyguard. It was a great experience, and we are all still very close friends. They all really got a kick out of my uncle and cousin showing up with their own entourage of about fifteen. My uncle Vincho took the entire crew out on a boat for the day. It was awesome, and from there, I was completely involved with Massachusetts and the MVMA. As a matter of fact, at one of the yearly meetings, Bob showed a video of our trip, and afterward, people I hadn't seen in a long time were coming up to me. Some were students at Tufts when I was working there as a technician, and they were happy to see that I had made it. Some were still confused, saying, "Wait a minute. Dan, are you a vet or a technician?" In any case, Ellen and I were feeling good back in Massachusetts after the relocation.

Bob introduced me to other MVMA board members, like Carlos Silvera, who was chair of the ethics committee. I eventually became very active in the MVMA as years passed. I was actually chair of the ethics committee for a year and was on that board for four years. While running the practice in Franklin, we were raising two young boys. I wonder how the hell I did it. No regrets at all.

I paid my dues and realized how crazy people are. I intervened in many frivolous lawsuits against a few colleagues, and it was always a very painful situation. I still think back about how things have changed for me, from my being a hellraiser of a kid to actually being chair of the ethics committee for the state of Massachusetts. Pretty amazing.

I started a job in the south shore of North Dartmouth with a spay and neuter outfit working on feral cats or cats of owners of "lower income." I took the job because it was a way to relocate. They paid me $55,000 a year with all the benefits. I accepted the job with the understanding if I finished my surgeries, I could leave and do relief work as a clinician. It was agreed at first, and then things started to change. They didn't realize that I was able to spay and neuter at least thirty cats between 8:00 a.m. and noon. It didn't sit right with the organization. I also became very suspicious when these "low income" owners were dropping off cats from their BMWs and Mercedes. I was also making a lot of noise in the area with the local veterinarians.

I had Carlos Silvera on my side. He is the owner of the Fall River Animal Hospital and was fifteen minutes away. He was also still running the ethics committee. Within the first two months, I received an invite for coffee at the nearest vet practice to where my place of employment was. It was basically a meet and greet, but it was with all the other surrounding vet practice owners. They wanted to see what I was about and who this guy—meaning me—cutting into their revenue was. It was pretty comical, as I remember it. I walked in as cool as a cucumber. I was very confident and casually answered all the questions, like "How many cats are you spaying?" I was able to spay a cat in eight minutes and neuter one in ten seconds. I basically said, "Hey! They are paying me fifty-five thousand a year with full benefits and a four-week paid vacation. If any of you can match it, I will be happy to hop on board." I think I left many with their jaws dropped. I was very confident and presented things in a matter-of-fact way.

As time moved on, I was getting eager to get back to working at a clinic. I ended up leaving the job and took a job in another local practice that lasted less than six months. I had worked with so many veterinarians and veterinary practices by this point I knew this wasn't for me. The owner and I split; I don't remember if I quit. I did give my two- or three-week notice. The owner was convinced that I needed to give a three-month notice. That was a huge laugh for me, but the owner was not laughing. She ended up screaming and jumping up and down like a crazy woman. I walked out and was thinking, *Is there anyone normal out there?* This owner was also a classmate of Sydell's and knew my situation. We have seen each other at meetings and have been very respectful and cordial. We both have our own very successful practices. It's pretty funny how things are handled in the heat of the moment. You learn as you get older to manage tempers and emotions a bit more easily. I immediately drove to Carlos's practice in Fall River and told him what the hell had just happened. We went out to eat at a great Portuguese place and had some drinks. I was working at Carlos's and some other practices for steady relief work. Ellen was still working at Tufts, and thank God we were on her health plan. She was just as happy as I was that I made the move to leave.

Franklin, Massachusetts, home of the first public library, was home for the Castillo family and the Franklin Vet Clinic family.

While I was at the practice I walked out of, I spent the last month sending out résumés to local practices and to practices I saw in the MVMA newsletter that were looking to hire an associate. I followed my old ways. I visited each practice personally to hand deliver them. I eventually got a call from my future boss. I would become a minority shareholder partner and eventually the sole owner of the Franklin Veterinary Clinic in Franklin, Massachusetts. I started as a junior associate in October of 1996. I was still living in Norton, and Franklin was about twenty minutes up 495. It was a very small practice, and the owner had just let one of his associates go. He started it from scratch in 1993 and had already seen multiple vet associates come and go in a very short time. I knew for some reason deep down, this was where I was going to plant my stakes. If it didn't work out here, I was going to start my own practice with absolutely no money or plan. After so many years of struggle and bouncing around, I planned on staying under any circumstances. I was thirty-four years old and had lived in four states and two countries. I wanted to have a place for me and Ellen, as we were trying to start a family.

It started out well. The owner and I had the same philosophy of practice: take care of the owners and their needs, and do whatever you have to do to fix the problem. Communicate constantly with the owners, and make yourself available. We worked this little matchbox of a practice from morning to night, just the two of us with a staff of about five or six. It was the time of beepers for emergencies. I had one week off and the next on. If I got beeped on a Sunday, I would go in and deal with the patient on my own without any technical support. I did many surgeries on my own back in the day, something that is unheard of nowadays.

I remember meeting Mr. and Mrs. Cusson with their white boxer, Noah, who had a spool of dental floss coming out of his mouth. I did that sedation, anesthesia, and surgery, a gastrostomy, solo. The owners and my boss were very happy. I built up my clientele very quickly, and within the first year, Ellen and I were about to put a bid on our first home.

By early 1997, things were going well at the job, and after many years of trying to have a baby, we finally were able to conceive. We tried for years, and with the help of professionals, we were blessed. Not only were things difficult with the struggle professionally but now with this. It was a difficult time at that age, as we were getting older and all our friends and family were having babies. I felt especially bad for Ellen with all the baby showers she would attend and all the christenings. A miracle happened, and we were able to conceive. We were all so happy. We of course decided not to tell anyone until it was safe, at the twelve-week mark. At twelve weeks to the day, we planned a trip to New York to visit family and decided to announce the news at my aunt Mary's house during a holiday Christmas party. After a toast of champagne, everyone at the party was elated. Within five minutes, I heard Ellen was in the bathroom and having a miscarriage. It was a horrible experience. The house was emptied in thirty seconds, and all left in shock. Ellen and I had to go back to my parents' apartment and try to get through one of the worst nights ever. It was horrible. We left early the next morning to meet her OBGYN at Framingham Union Hospital, where she confirmed the worst, no heartbeat. All people could say was that they were sorry. We were devastated. However we continued to move forward and our first son Austin was born July 26, 1998.

A few red flags with my boss were starting to arise at work. He was a real introvert, very quiet, and you didn't know where he might be coming from. He and his wife are really good people, but the warning signs were apparent. However, we got along great from a medical and surgical point of view. One time, as Ellen and I were putting a bid on our first house, I needed to leave during lunch to do a final walk-through. It took me a bit longer to return, maybe five to ten minutes. The next day, he said, "Hey, Dan, I need to talk to you." He said something to this effect: If I returned late from lunch, then all his employees would return late. That ate me up. I was producing over $300,000 for him, more than he had ever seen, and he came at me with this?

I had learned enough over the years and said, "Okay, no problem," but I was furious. By the way, putting a bid on our first home was something that happened quickly. Ellen and I went to a AAA meeting for first home buyers, where they had consultants and realtors to guide you. It seemed the $5,000 we had in our bank account provided enough to buy. We bought a house two miles from the practice. That was a sign for my boss as well that I had no plans to leave, or if I did, I would practice in the area. I believe the house was $180,000. It was a Cape Gambrel on 2.3 acres of land. It was a great starter home. This home was my first purchase that provided me income and leverage that would eventually come in a few short years. I was also late to the game as far as being a home owner. I was thirty-five years old. Both our boys were born there, as we lived there for seven years. It's where I built up the equity and leverage for what was about to come. It is where I also built up my clientele, as I would see everyone in town, in church, in the restaurants, and in the stores. I was out there. Most clients were having kids while we were all becoming friends as well. Austin was born in July of 1998 and Carter in February of 2000.

The difference in style between my boss and me were apparent. It really worked for the practice. We were not friends outside the practice. He was chasing his own kids around, and I was starting my family. We were not close. When Ellen was at least seven months pregnant, no one at the clinic even knew. I wanted it that way after one red flag after the next. Dr. Rob McCarthy from Tufts was at our practice one morning and blurted out, "Hey, Dan, Ellen is looking mighty pregnant." Ellen worked with Rob at Tufts. The staff and my boss were shocked. It was just one of those things he would do that would piss me off. He wasn't a communicator. Okay, did you say I am getting a raise, or is this a bonus? Or I can't take this time off?

One time, there was a local newspaper article about the practice. It was all about him, not one mention of me or any of the staff. I brought it to his attention. He hemmed and hawed, and I said nothing, but he knew exactly where I was coming from. I will give another example of how different things were. When Austin was born, the waiting room was full of clients and gifts for my family. Those same clients didn't even know that my boss had kids, and he was still living in Franklin at that time.

Soon, I started to get recognition in local newspapers and the MVMA. Articles appeared in the larger papers as well, like "Local Vet Lending a Hand in the DR." There was never a shouting match or a heated discussion. We worked well together and grew a small practice to a somewhat medium-size one.

Chapter 15

The Art of No Money Down

By 1999, I was engaging in discussions with him to do a buy-in. This is where things got fun and all should take note. I asked and asked again very politely, but I never got a real answer. I eventually connected with a couple of realtors and started looking at some locations to start a practice with not a pot to piss in. Again, I was doing all this with absolutely no money. This time, I also had a new baby at home. At that time, I received somewhat of a desperate call from my boss.

"Are you starting your own practice?"

I said, "Yes, I plan to do so, and I asked you multiple times to buy in and never got an answer."

"Oh no, Dan. We can work something out."

I had already been working at Franklin for about three years and had a huge following. I was producing a substantial lifestyle for him. By the way, I was still only making $55,000 with no benefits, as I was on Ellen's benefit plan from Tufts. So he had a real good thing going and didn't want to lose it. After weeks or perhaps months of preparing to do a buy-in, I was basically at my boss's will or direction on how he wanted to do it. We first started off with getting an appraisal of the practice. This was an appraisal for the business only, not the real estate. The practice was appraised by a well-known group out of Boston. I actually suggested them to my boss, as they were very reputable. I spoke with them and got some key information that I would use later on. The appraisal of the business came in at $400,000—not much but it was a small practice basically run by two vets and a handful of staff. My boss came up with a 30 percent buy-in. After going back and forth, I basically agreed because I had no other option. I also was adamant about becoming a 50/50 or 51/49 percent partner. He would not put that in writing. That was my first mistake. When I consulted with an attorney who happened to be a colleague's father, he basically said, "Dan, get your foot in the door. You have this opportunity, and it seems like a good deal. Take the 30 percent, and I am sure you will be in good shape."

We finally agreed, or shall I say, I had no other choice but the 30 percent buy-in of the business. This basically means you buy into 30 percent of profits. What were the profits? Well, that was whatever I was told in quarterly meetings with my boss and his brother, the accountant for the business. Now the most important part is coming up: 30 percent of $400,000 was $120,000. We went through all this work and costs, and I basically had no money, although my boss didn't know that. He also just wanted the money and was unwilling to cosign a note or provide any option to loan out of the business.

I started to get a bit stressed, thinking, *Where will I get $120,000?* I called the company that appraised the practice, and they gave me some leads. They were all shocked that I needed to borrow the money on my own and that the practice was not setting up some kind of plan for the buy-in. They all thought it was very strange. The one lead they gave me was a bank out of California that would advertise on the back of veterinary journals. I had been watching them for quite a while. They basically wired me a $120,000 loan in twenty-four hours. It had a 10 percent interest, and I was not able to make a balloon payment. It reminded me of the commercial I used to hear while growing up in New York. I believe it was from the former announcer of the New York Yankees, Phil Rizutto.

"Need money? Call the money store."

What else is one to do? I jumped on the loan, and the deal was done. It cost me $1,727 per month for ten years. Again, this was another stepping-stone to help me in the future for what would eventually happen. Thank God I had this opportunity. You always need to look down the road and have the vision of how one move will help or build a block for the next move.

About a month after the buy-in, when the ink was still not dry, my boss informed me in the middle of some conversation, "Yeah, Dan, we are going to keep you at 30 percent, and not plan to increase to 49 percent."

I was devastated but didn't let him know it. I may have asked what was going on, but I think I was so shocked and my heart sank so deep I just had no other response. I didn't have a response until I went home and told Ellen. I was so pissed, but I also had a mortgage, and I was looking at my year-old son, Austin. I couldn't make a move so carefree like I had for so many years. I could do nothing but just continue to go to work, suck it up, and build my clientele. I was becoming more known, and I was seen out and about town, while my boss took the money from the buy-in and eventually moved out of town about eight to nine miles away. We also basically changed our salaries to 100 percent percentage pay, I believe at 20 percent, which means I got a substantial boost in my pay, plus the bonuses from the buy-in. I was probably making about $75,000 to $80,000. I was doing okay, but I had my guard up and did not trust the guy. Anyone who can go back on their word is not worth it. So I continued to look and keep in touch with colleagues. I even worked as a relief vet for Carlos and a friend of mine down in Fall River on my days off. That move did not sit well with my boss, but it was about forty-five miles away from Franklin, so there was no conflict. It just sent a message that I was known, I needed to make money on the side, and in some way, I was keeping my options open.

Life was also moving on. Ellen and I were now expecting our second son, Carter, on February 7, 2000. Life was busy. We were working and raising the boys, who are eighteen months apart. Our lives were simple. The house was close to the practice, and I was able to pop over and help Ellen out even if it meant taking the boys for a walk in the double stroller with our crazy dog Lobo. Ellen stopped working at Tufts after Carter was born, and I was able to get on the health plan at the practice. In a typical day with two young babies at home, you don't do much. I tell the story to many new parents that a day for Ellen and me would be something like this. If I worked until 4:00 p.m. on a Saturday, I would meet her at the open house of a brand-new Dunkin' Donuts down the street. She would be waiting for me with the kids bouncing around among the clowns and balloons, celebrating the grand opening.

I was embedded into my new town of Franklin. I was very much into the community. On Sundays after church, I would run into clients and friends. If we went out to eat with the kids, I was always running into a client. I was also getting write-ups in local newspapers, regarding relief work in the Dominican Republic, or volunteering for one cause after another. I was also still involved with the MVMA and wrote a couple of articles regarding ethics and the grievance committee. In the summer of 2001, we took one of our trips up to Prince Edward Island, where my in-laws are from. That September, on the eighth, I took my brother-in-law Kevin down to New York to a Red Sox–Yankees game. It was a great night with him, my dad, and my cousin, Nicky. Kevin saw me in a much different light, especially working my way through the Bronx and upper Manhattan, speaking Spanish to everyone.

On the way back that night, after the game, we drove to Staten Island to sleep at my parents' house. As we were cruising on the BQE (Brooklyn Queens Expressway), we could see the Twin Towers hovering over us and the East River. It was an amazing night.

My cousin Nicky made a statement from the backseat: "This city is ready for another terrorist attack, but these buildings and the city are protected and you can't get within a mile radius." He did add that the city was just a target. Nicky just so happened to be in the Towers during the truck bomb that went off years earlier. We got back to Staten Island, had a great night, and then headed back to Massachusetts the next day but stopped up in Ossining at a friend's house for the day. It was a great weekend, something you don't get to do at all with young babies in tow.

Chapter 16

Ground Zero Shift, October 9, 2001

Everyone knows where he or she was during 9/11. As a New Yorker and especially being right down there three days before and having so many family members in and around the area, I had a deep connection. I was performing a surgery when I overheard a technician say she just heard a plane had struck one of the Twin Towers. I thought it must be a mistake but immediately knew my cousin Nicky was in one of those buildings.

As we all gathered around this little piece-of-crap black-and-white TV, we could see the tower smoking. I thought it was a small craft that had lost its way. Within minutes, we all witnessed the second plane hit the other tower. I was so naïve I was still thinking it must be a control tower issue and could not believe it was intentional. I started to call family members to see if they had heard from Nicky. Within the next hour, the buildings started to fall, and all of my thoughts were that Nicky was gone. There was no way anyone would survive. I started to call everyone, and no one had any information. It wasn't until about four to five hours later my cousin Marylou called the clinic, and the first words she said were "Danny, he got out." We both lost it and cried uncontrollably. The staff was all around and started to get upset. It doesn't stop the public. Most are good, but there is always that someone who wants his or her problems fixed. That was the case that day. Someone really didn't care what was going on! This person wanted their cat, who happened to be constipated, fixed. It was a long day and night.

As a matter of fact, one of my sons fell that day, and we had to run to the emergency room to have his cut chin patched up. It was a long night, and the next morning, my cousin Nicky called. When I heard his voice, I lost it again. He said as soon as he felt the building shake, he took off and ran down twenty-five flights of stairs, while others took their time or stayed in their seats. He ran out onto the streets, saw people jumping, and kept running. He saw and heard the second plane hit, and it seemed like they gunned it as they were approaching closer. He ran, I believe, almost to Midtown and stayed in a bar all night, as he could not leave Manhattan. He mentioned to his mom, my aunt Sissy, "What do you think, you raised an idiot? I ran until it felt like someone had poured a bucket of water on me."

I soon found out that I had multiple cousins and family members in the area. They were among the ones you see crossing the Brooklyn Bridge covered in ashes. My cousin's husband, Jim Cox, took the ferry back to Staten Island, and as it pulled away, one of the towers fell, and all to downtown Manhattan disappeared. He described that on the ferry it was a scene from the *Titanic*, pure chaos. I went down to New York that next weekend and took the ferry with Nick and my brother-in-law Steve. It was a very sad sight and situation. I felt I just needed to go down and see it. I reached out to friends I grew up with who were in the New York area to see how they were doing. I reached out to my old girlfriend who helped me through the tough years in the DR. I wrote a letter to her old address to say I hoped she and her husband and kids were safe. She called me days later and said they were. I lost it.

I found out about a list you could put your name on to go and help with the search and rescue dogs down at Ground Zero. I did and thought nothing of it. On October 5 or so, I got a call saying they had received my name to volunteer. I immediately said that I was unavailable. I was looking at my young boys and Ellen and wasn't sure it was the best idea. I then immediately called them back and said I was ready to go do whatever they needed. I received written instructions on what to bring, wear, and have on hand as I was to report on October 9 at 11:00 a.m.

I was to dress officially in scrubs with a stethoscope and pack light, not too many personal belongings. I had to bring my passport and any other ID I might have. I left the night before to drive to Staten Island. The day before that, American troops were landing in Afghanistan. New York City was in a complete lockdown with the National Guard and NYPD armed to the teeth all over the place. As I was about to cross the George Washington Bridge to get on the New Jersey Turnpike, there was a roadblock, and I was instructed not to stop but to drive without slowing down. The bridge was a target as well. If you think about it, if the George Washington Bridge ever goes out of commission, the entire eastern seaboard could shut down from Maine to Miami. That would be a major blow to the entire economy. I was nervous driving down to New York, especially with a war going on. There were so many unknowns that were out there, and everyone was on edge. As I approached the latter part of the turnpike, I could see downtown Manhattan still in flames. The pile smoked for almost six months, it seemed.

As I approached exit 13 to cross the Goethals Bridge, it was amazing the politeness of all the drivers. Everyone was letting everyone cut in front of them. It was a nice time. I don't know what happened to us since then. I arrived at my parents' house, ate some pizza, and tried to sleep, but I kept thinking about what was ahead the next day. My parents dropped me off at the ferry, and as we approached Manhattan Island, we could see the intensity, sadness, and shock in all. I made my way on foot to Ground Zero and asked some NYPD officers for exact directions.

As I got closer, they made way for me, and all lined up on each side of the road were cheering. One firefighter yelled, "Hey, the doc is here for the dogs! Let him through!" I almost lost it but couldn't because it was like I was on stage. I managed to keep it together. The cops were awesome. So was the National Guard, but for the cops and the FDNY, this was their turf. They knew every nook and cranny of the streets, and I followed their lead. It was noisy at times, very smoky, and then with a mild wind, the smoke would clear. It was ashes from the pile that was still burning. I found my way to the vet MASH unit located a block or two away from the pile on I believe West Street, but I was not so sure. I was welcomed by a young female vet who had just done the overnight shift and was leaving to catch a flight to Israel. I thought to myself, *She is one brave individual.* I did ask her if she was nervous about flying, and she seemed to just smile and shrug it off.

I was paired up with a veterinarian out of Connecticut. He was awesome. It was just the two of us for the next twelve hours along with the NYPD guarding the unit. We got to spend a lot of time together all of us. Unfortunately, we did not keep in touch. The shift started with getting to know the other veterinarian and the police officers. We were able to walk around and see the devastation and the look of shock in most everyone's eyes. I remember hearing the loud noises of the construction and then it going completely silent. That indicated that they had found the remains of a body. It was silent, and two by two, they would march the remains down the pile until the horn blew, and they would start up again. This went on and on for my entire twelve-hour shift. When the firefighters had a shift change, they would march right in front of our MASH unit. The cops informed us we needed to stand up at attention. They were literally about ten feet from us. It was hard to fight back tears. The cases that came into the MASH unit were few. Most of the cases were bandaging burned paws and listening to the police officers talking about whether the dogs got any "hits" today, meaning found any remains. They talked about how the dogs would go into a depression at not finding any survivors. The cops would have to play games and play hide-and-seek to keep them motivated.

At one point, we broke for lunch and went over to a large tent that the Red Cross had set up. As we were eating, along with firefighters and police officers, they had social workers walking around, asking if anyone wanted to talk. I was asked and said no, as I was only there for a twelve-hour shift. One young cop from Long Island asked if he could talk and open up. He went into the story of day one, describing the absolute chaos of that day that went on for about three days until there was more control of the situation at what is now called Ground Zero. All the leaders were dead, so a lot of shouting out of orders was common.

First body parts were to be placed on the piers on the Hudson: arms with arms, legs with legs. As the day went on, seagulls started to come and fly away with the parts. Logistically, it was a mess. Where did one go to relieve oneself? Defecate on this corner, and urinate on that corner. It was an amazing experience in general, seeing the unity of every citizen down there at that time from all over the world. Everyone I met was thanking me and asking how I could be helped. At about 9:00 p.m., two hours before my shift was to end, there was a group of EMC NYPD police officers sprinting toward me with a box in hand, yelling for help. My colleague and I were taken aback, as it was the real first action we had seen all day. I wondered what the hell could be in the box. When they opened it, a little baby finch bird was flopping around. They had seen it in the smoldering pile.

We sprang into action, offering the bird oxygen therapy as the police officers and firefighters were on their knees begging us to save it. The bird lived for about a week. I kept in touch with one of the officers from the unit, Anthony Favara, who lived in Staten Island, as did so many other officers and firefighters. Anthony and I became close, and I would look him up for a couple of years after 9/11 and bring down steaks and food for his unit, as well as some other firehouses on Staten Island, specifically Ladder 5, who lost, I believe, eleven guys. I did this out of gratitude. Then time went on and life got busy with the family, and things started to change.

It is very sad and upsetting to see the world and even our own country change and how we have become so divided.

The day after my shift, I went to visit my aunt Mary on Staten Island. She was the matriarch of the family after my grandmother passed away years before. She was so upset and would say, "I can't believe in my lifetime the world would be so sad and destructive." Here is a woman who saw a lot in her lifetime. She lost a brother in World War II. Her father, my grandfather, was in World War I, and her son was in Vietnam. I immediately responded, "This world is awesome and so are the people in it." What I saw at Ground Zero was an amazing example of the goodness of the world. The entire world was down there lending a hand. It was an amazing sight to see. I wish everyone could have witnessed it. What the hell happened to our country since then? Maybe the mistrust and too many wars for so long?

As I returned the next day, I stopped at a friend's house in Briarcliff, New York, on my way back to Massachusetts. She and her husband were having some major renovations to their house done, and it was full of workers. They gathered around and listened to my experience. We all seemed to be a bit shaken up as it was still so fresh.

I returned to Franklin and back to work, and all seemed to be very much interested in what I did. Local cops and firefighters and all had their own stories. Eventually, a local paper did a story on it as did the MVMA newsletter. I wasn't looking for the attention or interested in that one bit. It all just sort of happened.

My boss and I worked the practice very hard. Our families put up with a lot as well, as it was the time of emergency on call. Back in those days, we did one week on and one week off. Every Friday, we would pass off the beeper, and we would cover emergencies for the entire week. I have had many interruptions in family occasions, including Christmas and other precious times that I didn't want to miss. The blessing was I was so close to work I would be back home before you knew it.

I was talking to one of my sons about this, and he mentioned he remembered me leaving in the middle of the night to see a sick pet. We did everything in those days. I have done many surgeries alone with no help many times. It just doesn't exist anymore with the newer generations of veterinarians. They need too much support around them, whether it is equipment or staff. That is not a bad thing either, especially nowadays with the liability issues. No longer or seldom can you make a mistake without some type of a threatening letter or lawsuit. He and I worked the practice very well and had a good working relationship. The only thing that was in the back of my mind was my future. I wasn't satisfied being held at the 30 percent ownership level.

Chapter 17

Hold Your Cards Close

It was the end of spring of 2001, perhaps June. I was to meet with my boss and his brother to review the last quarter. I thought it was nice they did that with me, but they might as well have been speaking Chinese. His brother was a numbers guy and basically said, "Here it is. This is what is, and here is your check after all expenses are paid." I was no idiot, and I knew the expenses were minimal. The building and facility were run down, old, and maybe a thousand square feet. It had a house on the property as well that used to be rented out but was now converted. There was a surgical unit where a living room once was. As I talk to my staff now, I call it "back in the old days in the piece-of-shit building."

By the time this meeting was about to take place, it was on my mind to bring up again my situation of the 30 percent and how that was never my goal. I was doing a couple of relief days down at the Cape for a friend's practice and had a half-thought-out plan. If worse came to worse, we could always relocate down at the Cape and buy out my friend's practice, as he was focusing more on equine medicine and surgery. His dad was the attorney who helped me with the 30 percent buy-in. At the end of the meeting, while they were gathering their belongings, I asked if they had a minute to put things on the table. I did it in a very calm manner but didn't know where it would all end. If they said no, that I needed to stay at 30 percent, it was a done deal for me. I would have to leave in the near future. This one statement or discussion changed the trajectory of life for me, my family, and many other families at the practice who are still with me after twenty years.

I said, "Hey, guys, I need to talk to you about my future. It was always my goal to be a 50/50 or 51/49 percent partner. I asked multiple times, and I am asking again. If that is not in your plan, that is fine, but I will be leaving for a practice down at the Cape." I was a little nervous, as I had *zero plans to go anywhere soon*. I had two babies at home, a new mortgage, and a wife who had supported me for so many years and was not really eager to do this bullshit all over again.

Their reaction was complete shock and bafflement. They initially were slack-jawed. They started to talk and let some very disturbing information out. It turned out that my boss had already purchased a piece of property in his hometown some eight miles away as the crow flies. He basically was planning to start another practice, without me, by the way. He would do the 51/49 percent split with me, but he would be working at the other practice and utilizing all the staff at Franklin. I believe I responded calmly and basically told them I didn't think that would work and now they owed me my 30 percent back. We all agreed to sleep on it, but as I drove home and told my wife, I thought, *What a piece of work! He must think I fell off the back of a truck. Let me get this right: he buys property, buys and coordinates a prefab building, and doesn't want me to be part of it? What kind of a partnership is that?* Certainly one that I no longer wanted any part of.

At this time, I had already established a team of an attorney and accountant/advisor. I connected with both of them throughout the year and knew all about them. I called them immediately the next day and explained what my situation was. As weeks passed, my boss and I managed to work and see cases as if nothing had happened. We continued to have a great work relationship.

Frank Muggia from Buffalo, New York, but originally from Winchester, Massachusetts, was one of the top attorneys in the country regarding veterinary medicine and buy-in and buyouts. Walter Abbot had a top-notch well-known accounting firm out of Arlington, Massachusetts, specializing in the veterinary field. Their expertise was what I needed. They have been with me for over twenty years now.

A few weeks later, I was on vacation up in Prince Edward Island and got a call from Frank. I remember standing on the deck at the cottage with a beer in my hand. I was explaining the entire situation, and he knew I had one choice. I needed to buy this guy out completely along with the real estate. At the end of the conversation, I asked Frank how much his service would be, as I didn't have a pot to pee in. He said that this might take a while, almost a year, and it would cost more or less around fifteen thousand. I had already started a relationship with Walter, and he also knew what needed to be done and had all the banks lined up for my needs.

As I returned from vacation and continued with multiple conversations with Frank, he suggested I get a letter of intent to push these guys, as nothing was getting done. He basically said, "Place this letter on his desk and never talk about the issues. Never let any conversations get heated or emotional." As days went on, we managed to continue to work cases and go about our business like we had not a worry in the world. The staff was unaware of what was happening at this point. They called for another meeting and were both really interested in who this attorney was, how much I was paying, and how I could afford it. I remained quiet and basically said, "If you don't sign the letter of intent, you now owe me the 30 percent back." Remember the 30 percent loan I took out of a magazine at 10 percent interest with no balloon payment? This loan that people thought I was absolutely nuts for taking was now working for me and giving me all the leverage I needed. The last thing they wanted was to pay me back $120,000 and on top of that have me leave the practice, especially with what I had established over five years. This really got things going, and they started to lawyer up and get the process going.

At first, and for a while, it was a complete game. Their proposals were, "Well, I will sell you 70 percent and keep the real estate" or I would be a 90 percent owner and get half the real estate. After a while, with Frank's encouragement, I said, "I will buy you out 100 percent of the business and 100 percent of the real estate. If not, I am walking." To where I would be walking, I had no clue at the time. And I would buy 100 percent of the business and property with what money, I also had no clue.

The game was on, and we had to get the practice and the real estate appraised again. This was all in process, and I knew it was going to be a long process. We managed to keep the business going and continued to work it as if nothing else was happening. I started to receive some invoices from Frank. I took a line of credit out of our home for fifteen thousand. This was specifically set up in the Frank Muggia account. I was wheeling and dealing with no money of my own. By the time I bought out the practice, it was appraised at $800,000, and the real estate was about $400,000. After many complaints of the appraisals from the other side, saying they came in too low, I basically just ignored them. They were also trying to come up with goofy formulas; for instance, they could keep clients and have them go to his new practice. It was a complete shit show. Thank God for Frank telling me to keep cool. The plug could have been pulled anytime if I pissed them off, and I would have been left stranded. It was also going to be an issue borrowing all this money with the owner starting a new practice about eight miles away. I would say my boss and his brother did connect with a bank to do the deal out of Taunton, Massachusetts. So things were working. At this point, we wanted it to go and just move on, but it was a stressful time. For about the last six months we were working together, I would ask my boss to show me how to use the computer and how to pay bills, as I had absolutely no clue. He would just say, "Don't worry about it," and that he would show me. During the process, I believe they were impressed with the team I had. They would ask if I had a new business account registered with the state of Massachusetts and about other items that needed to be done. I would respond, "Check, check! All taken care of thanks to Walter Abbott and Frank."

The date for the closing was set for May 17, 2002. Things were getting a bit tense but were still manageable. We had an issue with a staff member's daughter who was taking drugs out of our drug cabinet. I heard about it from another staff member, a kid named Brian, who was a high school kid at the time. He was at a local party, and he overheard that our practice was being hit by this staff member's daughter, who was working with us after school. My boss said, "Dan, you need to address this," as I was about to buy him out in the next two to three weeks. It did not go over well at all with either of the girl's parents, whom, by the way, we had known for years and spent many Christmas parties with. The dad met me and my boss one morning and was completely defensive. He basically threatened to take legal action against us and mentioned something about Brian, the kid who was still working for us. Brian was found one night at work in the other building lying on the floor drunk. I heard about it the next day and had a heart to heart with him. I said I wouldn't tell his parents, but he needed to be careful because next time he would be finished. After the meeting with the girl's dad, my boss said, "We have no choice but to let Brian go."

I responded, "You didn't want to get involved with the girl, but now you want to fire Brian? If you want to fire him, go right ahead, as I will rehire him after our closing."

Brian eventually stayed, and now after multiple community colleges and colleges and a master's out of Harvard, he is very successful with his family and has multiple homes. He is one individual that I am so proud of. He was a bit like me. It didn't come easy, but he kept going and just needed a chance.

About the last two months before the closing, the staff and certain clients found out. I was aware that my boss was letting clients know, although he was legally obligated not to do so. I was just wondering most of the time which staff members would follow him. Whom could I trust? But I didn't let it get to me too much, as I was focused on May 17.

At this point, I was also not being let in the loop on how to pay or even look at an invoice. I kept thinking, *Well, maybe tomorrow he will show me.* About three days before the closing, we were having computer issues. He would try to fix things himself, but it was always a shit show. The computer system was down. I would sit in reviews with staff, and he would go into this long, mumbling tangent. At the end of the meeting, the staff member would pull me aside and ask, "Dr. Castillo, am I getting a raise?"

I would just shake my head and say, "I have no freaking clue."

He would go on about how much the payroll taxes were. We lost two long-term employees months before our closing. The morning of the closing, all were very nervous, no doubt. It was scheduled at a local attorney's office at 11:00 a.m., which meant we had to close appointments and Ellen needed to get coverage for the boys. My boss came in with about eight large boxes of invoices and bills and said, "Here you go. It's easy to do. Don't worry about it."

As we all arrived at the attorney's office, there must have been about eight people around this very large conference table. My banker slammed his hand on the table and gave a warning to my boss and his brother. "If there is anything new or something crazy comes up, I am walking." It was pretty intense. What had happened up until then always had to do with the noncompete clauses. They were always pushing the envelope. As a matter of fact, we had a three-year agreement that he needed to pay me a certain percentage of existing clients that followed him. I didn't trust them for the life of me. After about two hours of signing documents, we all stood up and shook hands, and my last words were "Thank you very much for the opportunity," and I handed him a check for $1.3 million. The $1.3 million was the amount of the business and the real estate. Ellen and I walked out, hugged in the parking lot, and planned to meet at the house later on. When I got home, she was there with our two close neighbors, Bob and Gina, waiting with champagne to celebrate. It was a huge relief but a bit overwhelming to say the least. A loan for $1.3 million when everything is riding on you between family at home and the work family?

The first stop on the way back to the practice was a local computer store. I knew the computers were down, and I had no time to fuck around. Steve, the computer guy, was there in a short while the next day, but it took three days to fix the problem.

As I approached the practice, there were three staff member waiting with open arms and hugging me. They said, "You did it! Congratulations! You did it." Those three staff members, Loren, Pam, and Cathy, remained with me, although Cathy retired last year. I knew at that point my foundation of the practice was built, and they had no plans to jump ship and follow my boss. As a matter of fact, there was not one staff member who followed him.

After celebrating the first night, I had to face reality. Computers were down, and all were in a panic. I basically in a calm manner advised all to take out papers and pens and start getting clients' information and credit card information. I mentioned, "I will be dammed if this glitch is going to stop me." We did this for about two full days and managed to receive all payments. After twenty-five years, there is always a computer glitch, and I haven't changed: take down the information, and keep working. I do not need a computer to look at a dog or cat. I also had to deal with paying bills and invoices, something I have never in my life experienced. It would take me hours at night to see which vendor needed payment. I had no clue what a thirty-day invoice was or whom to pay it to. I was handwriting all my checks. Payroll was interesting, but the company, which is still with me now, has been awesome. Jim Fox from Fox Payroll was a huge help. I just continued to work and see patients. All was coming back to me from my experiences. At my first job for $3.35 an hour, my mentor Dr. Tom Carreras always used to say, "Don't worry about the money. Just keep working, and all will fall into place. Keep practicing good medicine, and bills will get paid." What has happened in the last ten years or so is that all the new veterinary graduates are getting these condensed business classes in vet school. It's a very good subject to have in veterinary school, but it is somewhat misguided.

The reality is that time is money. If a graduate is not willing to put the time in when he or she realizes that this job is not a nine-to-five job, he or she may have chosen the wrong career. I guess one big change is that today's veterinarians are not putting in the hours that we used to. You can generate just so much money on a thirty-five- to forty-five-hour workweek. You need to put the extra time in, staying after hours on the phone or seeing emergencies and going the extra mile. I am not saying that today's veterinarians are not working hard; it's just a different mind-set. I have interviewed many candidates, both veterinarians and veterinary technicians. What I see now is that the tables are somewhat reversed. It almost has become an interview process where I am the one getting interviewed. I usually sit back and let them ask everything about our practice. They will ask schedules, quality time, benefits, and salary. Then I usually turn the tables and say, "Okay, what is it that you think you bring to my practice? How will the practice benefit from having you and your skills? ... Oh really? You haven't performed much surgery? Or you need help with surgery? It takes you an hour to do a cat spay, and for me and other associates, it takes twelve minutes, and you want how much a year at what type of work schedule? ... Oh, you can't work more than one night a week or one Saturday a month?"

You see where I am going with this? The industry has changed and in some ways not for the better. There is a corporate influence now in our profession, and they are buying practices like ours all the time. With that being said, the community setting is scarce. It becomes a vet in the box—multiple vets changing all the time with no real community connection. Protocols on how to treat a patient are documented and followed strictly by a business manager or hospital director who is following the order of a business manager.

As weeks became months of owning the practice, all became somewhat more of a routine. I have often said that one thing that caused me the biggest anxiety was sitting in the parking lot and wondering, *What if none of my staff members show up?* I knew how to treat patients but didn't know how to book an appointment on the computer. As a matter of fact, twenty-five years later, I still don't know how to book an appointment. It's amazing how things fall into place. Walter Abbott and the accounting firm, as well as economic advisors, stood by me and walked me through tax issues. Then I would really see staff members take control, something I didn't see when I was in the partnership. The staff members never had the opportunity to perform, and I gave them the green light to do so. I learned quickly, and maybe it was because I worked in so many places, that you need to let the people around you grow and fly. This has been a big asset for me and the practice. Stay out of micromanaging, delegate, form the culture, and lead, and as that culture forms, it acts as the foundation and example for all other new members. Some try to fight it and go against it. At times, I may have taken too long to respond and ask them to leave, but once the culture is set, it becomes the identity of the practice. Be personable, help the client, help each other, and always have some kind of an outlet outside work. Having an outlet outside of work is so important in every business but especially this one.

Most people don't realize, but veterinary medicine has one of the highest suicide rates; if not the highest, it is near the top of the list. There are many reasons. Compassion fatigue is one. This happens primarily from multiple euthanasias or not being able to save a patient. With this, you need to go from one exam room to the next upbeat and positive for a family with a new pet, right after you euthanized a patient from a family that you may have known for years. Most recently, in the last fifteen to twenty years or so, another reason is the economic burden that the profession requires. Some new veterinarians are coming out of school with over $300,000 in student loans.

The other factor is the public scrutiny and pressure. Times have changed, and the public is much more demanding and less forgiving—it is even threatening at times. I have managed this pretty well, and perhaps it's because I think I saw the worst that could happen in my early career back in Virginia with the Katz family.

Within the first year, the practice was moving into the little shit building that I bought and tried my best to spruce up with paint, murals, a cleaner look, and lighting. I was also setting the tone and creating the culture with three specific staff members, two of whom are still with me: Cathy, who just retired in July of 2019; Loren, and Pam. I was getting used to interviewing and hiring new staff and at times, although sometimes too late, letting people go. One person can definitely intoxicate the entire machine, and that person needs to go.

I was also very protective of my investment and still am. I always had to have my eyes behind my back at my former partner, whose practice was up and running less than ten miles away. If it wasn't one thing, it was another. A client came in one day and said our phone number was going to the Franklin Pizza and Deli in the phone book. So I called my former partner on it, and his response was he must have given the wrong number to the phone book company. So I called my attorney, Frank, about it, and he confronted them with a letter. Their response was that I was being petty. Frank responded with, "Well, Dan just paid $1.3 million and has every right to protect his investment." Nothing could have been done at that point, but I did go over to the Franklin Pizza and Deli. I introduced myself, took all their menus, and passed them out at the clinic. They did the same for me, and twenty-five years later, we are all clients of each other's and are still helping and referring.

One day, I saw my partner's truck in Franklin with a sign advertising his veterinary clinic house call service on it. I called him immediately and said, "Knock it off, and take off the sticker while in Franklin." We both paid quite a bit for attorneys at our closing, and we were both on a noncompete agreement for three years. I held him to it until the last day.

While I was dealing with all of this and raising the kids with Ellen, my mind was always on the move for the next phase. I knew in my mind I was not going to continue to practice in this small building of possibly one thousand square feet. I started to do my homework and talk with multiple builders and members on the planning boards, just to get some ideas about a massive addition to the practice. I was doing this while every morning, I would check my emails from clients, friends, and realtors about moving into a bigger house. My mind was always thinking about the next step. I knew we were not going to be able to compete in this building for much longer. It was old and very tight.

Chapter 18

Monopoly Money

The year was 2004. It was two years after the purchase of the practice with its property, and I was about to go a bit crazy, taking a lot of risks most people would not have taken. I will call this chapter "Monopoly Money," or "Mo Money, Mo Money." I spoke with about four local builders, including a prefab company. I was comfortable with a builder named John Desmond and his business, Complete Development Corp. His proposal was about $600,000. We would eventually quadruple the size of the initial building. Through Walter, I started to look for a bank and eventually went to the bank that had just lent me $1.3 million two years prior. They were looking at me like I had two heads and eventually declined. They actually tried to persuade me to sit tight, being that I only had two years under my belt. We came to a disagreement, and I went with another bank, which also took my $1.3-million-dollar loan on as well as collateral. My original bank was not happy at all, but I needed to make a move right away and would not wait. The bank that I went with tried to convince me to move to another location and start with all new construction. I was adamant about staying right where we were located, being that the entire town knew the location, and it was right on a main road, State Road 140. It was less than a quarter mile from McDonald's. Location, location, location.

We started to coordinate the engineers and the building permits, and before we knew it, we were breaking ground the week of Thanksgiving in 2004. The roof was on by Christmas four to six weeks later. It was an amazing sight to see and very exciting for the staff and the clients. It was pretty amazing watching the contractors help the clients in and out of the door with their pets. We all literally became family as the project went on for eighteen to twenty-four months. We initially built it in two phases. Phase one was the first addition, which was finished on April 20, 2005. On Saturday, April 20, 2005, we worked until noon and then proceeded to move into phase two, the new building. It was an amazing feeling. That first addition is 3,500 square feet. There were so many details that I managed at this time. I was not only managing the project but also the computer systems, phone systems, shelving, and medical equipment. The medical equipment was very expensive and detailed: anesthesia machines, surgical lights, tables, scrub sinks—the list was long and very expensive, well over a hundred thousand. I was doing all this and seeing patients at the same time. We worked out of the new addition for about a year until I took another loan out and built phase two, which was the old building demolition and the rebuilding of that using the same footprint and having it all match phase one. In total, it is about 5,500 square feet. Today, this building is worth about $1.5 million.

Hold on, folks—this is where it gets really fun. What I did in 2004 is not for the wary. In June of 2005, as the contractors were starting to demolish the original building and construct phase two, I got a call from a friend/client/realtor to meet her ASAP at a house that just came on the market. For the last year or so, I would review emails with larger homes in the area. We started to outgrow our first home, which Ellen and I thought would be our home for life. We were there for seven years and remember it was our first home. I was a late bloomer, and I didn't own a home until I was thirty-five years of age. The next step up was your typical colonial home anywhere from 2,500 to 3,500 square feet. A home like this in 2004 was going for about $400,000 to $500,000. In the meantime, I was talking to my builder, John Desmond, who was doing all the work at the practice. We had a plan to do an addition at our house. The plans were all in the works, and I was going to manage two projects at the same time. I already was a year into phase one at the clinic, so I was comfortable with it. Austin, my oldest, was all registered for kindergarten in that district.

One morning, my friend Nancy, the realtor, sent an email about a house that just came on the market. She called me at work and asked that I meet her there at noon that day. This house was a bit different and was in a nice big neighborhood. It was 4,500 square feet, much bigger than the typical colonials I had been looking at in the last year. I went and met Nancy on my own without mentioning anything to Ellen. The house struck me as awesome, and it was perfect—much different than what we had been looking at. I immediately called John, who was at the clinic, and asked that he come right over, which he did. As John, Nancy, and I were walking through it, John started to measure things up and said, "The house is 4,500 square feet!" Then we realized there was a very large pool in the backyard completely landscaped. The sellers were asking for $604,000, which was totally out of my range—and remember, I didn't really have the funds for it. John turned to me and said, "Dan, take the house. Let's back off on the planned addition at the existing home."

I called Ellen, and she came over within minutes. I turned to Nancy and asked her to give me twenty-four hours but assured her we were interested. I then called Walter, and this is how things got done. Walter asked, "Dan, do you like the house?"

"Yes, we do!"

"How much?"

"Six hundred four K."

Walter's response was always cool and calm. "Well, Dan, this is what we are going to do. Six hundred four K is not that much over the span of a thirty-year loan. It is not a problem. Tell the realtor you're interested and get ahold of the seller."

As I left the house to see appointments that afternoon, I was in the driveway and ran into some neighbors who all knew me, as I was their veterinarian. When they told me whose house it was, I discovered it happened to be owned by a client I had known for quite a while.

She called at the clinic that afternoon and said, "Dr. Castillo, are you the one interested?"

I responded, "Yes, but we literally just looked at it."

She said, "Well, no worry. I will have everyone back off."

She would wait to see what Ellen and I could do. It appeared that her husband had a high position with General Dynamics and needed to relocate down to DC. Later that night, I spoke with Walter, and we started to get into some details. He asked, "How bad do you want the house?" but was also very happy that John Desmond, the builder, approved. He really was a great and honest guy and lost on future income with our planned addition. Walter advised me to tell the seller and realtors we would buy the house without contingencies, meaning I was willing to buy it without needing to sell my house. Risky but it's the thing you do to back everyone off and position yourself first in line. You need to become a player and back everyone off.

I went to talk to Nancy to propose this to the sellers and said, "Let's get this thing going. Now all I need are the funds for a down payment."

Walter was able through contacts with banks to coordinate a bridge loan in order to come up with more funds and help pay off others. I was flying around like a crazy person, getting paperwork for the new house, putting our house on the market, and managing the clinic construction. At the same time, the town of Franklin was squeezing me and the builder for more funds for drainage in the parking lots and other matters that went way over my budget but I needed to pay in order to keep the doors open and keep income flowing. At that time, the banks were throwing money around. At one point, I had to ask them to stop. "I am good for now."

It literally became monopoly money. So when the town mentioned something like drainage tanks in the parking lot, I needed to do it. This was at the cost of about $60,000. I had the mentality to not slow down and keep the doors open.

Amazingly, our clients continued to walk through the doors in the middle of a construction site with their pets, and it all became the norm day in and day out.

I started to get a bit nervous when our house was not selling. There were a few curves that came out of left field that I had no control over. I wasn't expecting to put new siding on. The back of the house had been destroyed by a woodpecker. It was clapboard, and a woodpecker was going after insects, I guess. As a veterinarian, I felt guilty asking one of my staff members, Loren, if she had access to a BB gun. She said her son Nick had one, so she brought it to work the next day. I attempted to shoot it, but it was moving too fast. I wasn't expecting to put a new septic system in. In the state of Massachusetts, they have something called Title 5, which protects buyers of homes if the septic system needs to be replaced. Our home that we were showing looked like a bomb had hit it. We also had two young boys about four and five years of age. We had to leave the house many times so people could see it and say they were not interested. The house also had some mold up in the attic that needed to be dealt with. All of these renovations added up to about $30,000 to $40,000. I needed to pull money out of the letter of credit on the home. I had loans and money coming out of every orifice. I just kept plowing forward, seeing patients, and showing up to work ten to twelve hours a day, running home and checking on Ellen and the kids, and really having a good time with the whole thing. It really didn't stress me out too much.

Recently, I had dinner with the builder, John. He mentioned when he met me going through all this he would go home wondering how the hell I was keeping all of it together and not having my head explode. I was in a major routine. I'd get up very early 4:30 to 5:00 a.m., have coffee, read the news, and then head to work, always before anyone else arrived. I was also a workout junky, always doing something at the gym or with karate. The boys and I were heavily into Kenpo karate at the time. We were always on the move. Ellen was as well, and once the kids were old enough to get involved with organized sports, we were off from one activity to the next with me always either coaching or assisting coaching.

The old house eventually sold, I think for close to $300,000. We had bought it for $179,000. It sold right before our closing for the new house. We moved into the new house, which we still live in today. We moved in on Austin's sixth birthday, July 26, 2004. We had some moving trucks there, and before you knew it, we were all in the swimming pool in the backyard meeting and hanging out with the new neighbors. It's a great house and worth a lot more now. The best thing is that I was able to pay it off last year. It was a thirty-year mortgage, and I paid it off in fifteen years. It was no magic trick at all: hard work, discipline, paying more a month, and not living above our means for sure. Our lives were and are very much attached to the routine of the community, the practice, and our home.

A big day for us would be getting out of work and going to maybe Applebee's for dinner. We went to church every Sunday or Saturday night. I did lawn work and saw emergencies on weekends. I was always available to see clients off hours.

I had a beeper. Most people had my cell or home phone because we were so involved with the community, and everyone had a pet. Our vacations were either a trip down the Cape, renting a client's house or something very local, never too far out of the area.

The building of the practice sort of happened; it was not something I planned for. I always had at least one other veterinarian with me. Most of the time, we were three. With more veterinarians comes more staff, including a receptionist and veterinary technicians. The one thing that has always been consistent was our hours of operation. We have always been open 8:00 a.m. to 8:00 p.m. Monday through Thursday, until 5:00 p.m. on Friday, and until noon on Saturdays. We at times were open until 4:00 p.m. on Saturdays.

The culture of the practice or any type of business starts from the top, and it may take years of failing and trying different things. For me, it did take years. I definitely made mistakes, but you learn from them. The key is you need a team or small group to set that culture, and then that group increases, and years later, it happens. When there are new employees coming in, sometimes from another practice, we set the tone, although we are always willing to listen and take advice. I am at the point where there is no time for bullshit. Don't be late, and don't ever make a habit of calling in sick. I have people here who have been here for the last twenty years, and I could count on one hand how many times they called in sick.

I have been a jack of all trades and mastered cutting through the BS. Back in the day, I would do my own landscaping. I remember landscaping one Sunday on a very hot day and having to interview a new vet associate. She came and approached me while I was mowing the lawn. "I am here for an interview with a Dr. Castillo."

I responded, "That's me!"

She was awesome and took the job. She lasted about a year. She ended up getting married and moved to Rhode Island. We still see each other at meetings and laugh at some things I did. I remember scaring her to death on Halloween. She was here maybe a month, and I greeted her one morning coming up the stairs with a huge ax in my hand, dressed as a werewolf. It's part of the culture I was talking about. One Halloween tradition is scaring the shit out of staff members.

Today, I look back and see that really you learn to work smarter. My advisor/friend Walter Abbott would say, "Okay, Dan, how long does it take to do your landscaping? Just think how many pets you can see in that time."

He was right. I think about the place, and it looks better than ever because we have professional landscapers doing what they do. I now can focus on what I do. You work smarter and harder, not easier. You are always thinking about what you can do to get better.

I was getting used to maintaining the practice and paying the mortgages. I was always involved with the kids and their schools, giving talks for show-and-tell with a bunch of X-rays or doing fundraising. Thank God for my wife, Ellen.

She made it all possible. She was able to stay home with the boys from the time they were born through middle school. She did make it all possible for this whole thing to exist. Those are crucial years, and I think if economical, it is worth it to go with one income. Easier said than done for sure, but worth it.

Every penny I made was kicked back into the practice. Through Walter's advice, I drew a salary of less than $100,000 a year. The extra funds were for maintenance and repairs or whatever else there was. We started to take some vacations, and one big advantage was using the credit cards to buy medical supplies earned airline miles. At this point, I started to reconnect with the DR and would bring my father down as well, all in business class. It was amazing thinking not long ago I would be crying on the plane going back to school in the DR. Now I am going back established and seeing my family down there, who basically took me in and made a lot of this all happen. I took Ellen and the boys down when the boys were four and six years old and introduced them to a whole new world. We continue to travel there on a regular basis, excluding this time of COVID-19. As the practice and the system became more and more stable, we traveled farther. Disney World was a big one in 2010. The boys were in middle school. It was an all-out vacation, top of the line at the Beach and Yacht Club where we had a major suite. The money was there do to so, after saving it and managing it through the years, and this was the time for us as a family to relax.

I was always thinking in the back of my mind what my dad would say: "A time for work and a time for play," and I could do both very well. I started to plan bigger trips with the family, knowing that the boys were getting older. They were in high school and almost getting ready for college. We took trips to Jackson Hole, Yellowstone, Hawaii, and California that were amazing. The most memorable I would say were Barcelona, Spain, and Positano, Italy. There is no doubt that my Spanish comes in handy. It really helps, and I will never forget my cousin Jose in the DR saying, "Danny, you will leave this country with a degree and another language and another culture." We were able to travel through the Caribbean for leisure and at times for continuing ed. We visited the DR, Puerto Rico, Aruba, Turks and Caicos, and the Bahamas. For me, Cuba was the most memorable.

I got word from my friend Dr. Rob McCarthy, who is one of the professors at Tufts University. He was going to give a lecture for an organization representing veterinarians throughout Latin America. Havana, Cuba, was hosting. This was months before the Obama administration opened up the relationship, which has since then been shut down by the Trump administration. It was a six-month application process through the State Department. At any given time, you can be canceled up until two weeks before your proposed flight. It was a risk, but I wanted to go, knowing so much of the history of Cuba. I was accepted, and the next thing I knew, I was on a flight from Logan to Miami. I stayed at the Marriott at Miami airport.

The next morning, I took a flight on the far end of the airport to Havana.

How amazed I was knowing that in less than forty minutes, I would be in Cuba. If we could rewrite history, Cuba should have never closed off from the United States. To me, it's a shame getting to know the people, how desperate they were and how they wanted a change. I was greeted by a minivan with two guys, a chauffeur, and I assume a guard. I sat in the backseat, and by the time we exited the airport, I was completely in awe at the old cars, the organization, and the cleanliness. I then said in Spanish, "How is the Cuban beer?" The two guys turned around in complete shock.

"Oh my god," they were saying, "he is one of us."

They were so happy that I was able to communicate. I definitely received very good treatment. They loved me, and they took me all over to places I believe not your typical Canadian or European tourist would go. I absolutely loved it and hope one day this country will have the freedom it deserves.

As years went on, the practice grew at a very steady pace. The team and culture were set, and new additions of staff members either caught on, left, or were asked to leave. The team in place provided all, not just me, peace of mind, knowing while being away on a day off or a vacation that all would be okay. In the economic crisis of 2008–2009, things became a bit unsteady or unpredictable. I knew exactly what income needed to be generated on a daily basis and then a weekly basis just to cover payroll and bills, which did not let up. The industry of veterinary medicine was always considered recession proof. This was much different and very unsettling.

After about six weeks of decreased revenue, I called a meeting. I offered to lower all staffs' income by 10 percent, excluding veterinarians. I had all sign a document, and if they didn't sign, I would have to let them go. Every staff member signed on, and before you knew it, in eight to nine months, I was able to coordinate with my payroll company what income was lost by each staff member. This way, I was able to cut a check for all income lost for each staff member. People were shocked, and most are still here with me at the practice.

Investing money back into the practice was always on the horizon. It was more now than just a large building. If it was $20,000 to install a new computer system, we did it. Did we need $40,000 for a new digital X-ray machine? We did it. Lab equipment, surgical equipment, office supplies—it was always something and always worth it. By this time, we were a staff of about fifteen, with four full-time veterinarians. I was always able to coach the kids, run the lacrosse program, and eventually help coach their high school team. While all this was happening, Ellen went back to school for about two years and earned her degree as a respiratory therapist. She worked very hard driving to class an hour away and studying at night. She eventually passed multiple boards. It was definitely a crazy time, as the kids were not driving yet, and I was needing to leave work to drop them off and pick them up from their school about twenty-five minutes away. We managed to pull it off, and it was well worth it. It was very scary at the time, paying for that tuition, which was not cheap and was unexpected, but we somehow managed. We just kept plugging forward. There were no vacations at this time with Ellen in school. She just couldn't get the time off. So what I would coordinate would be long weekends to the Cape or New York City as an escape for all of us just to get a break. This way, she could study and then try to relax and not miss any school.

Chapter 19

Life and Death Decisions

The boys and I went with another friend of mine to Nantucket. Ellen did not go this time. We rented a house, just the dads and the kids. We were putting on a lacrosse camp for the week, which was a great time. I was able to get the sticker for my truck and drive on the beach called Surfside. It's another event in my life I will never forget, and I thank God for protecting me.

We were all hanging out on the beach after multiple games of volleyball. As we all set up our beach chairs and grabbed a couple of beers, we heard, "Help!" from a guy on the shore in desperate need of assistance. He was standing there with his surfboard. My friend, Jack, and I ran toward him, and he begged us to go and save his friend from drowning. We thought nothing of it but couldn't see his friend on the shore. He grabbed me, looked me dead in the eyes, and said, "Please take my board. You need to save him!" and pointed way out.

Jack looked at me and said, "Dan, I am not a strong swimmer."

The guy grabbed me again and said, "Please help him! Take my surfboard."

I turned around, and there were about thirty people standing in shock and not moving. In the back of my mind, I was thinking, *Someone else will jump in and do this, right?* As I looked across the horizon, I could see this head bobbing at least two football fields out in the ocean. I am not kidding, two hundred yards out. I don't know what took over me really. I grabbed the board, tied the rope around my ankle, and started to paddle out. The first part was very hard, as I was getting knocked back and forth in some very rough surf. I would get back on the board and try to go under the crashing waves. I finally got through the rough surf and then went into autopilot, paddling like a maniac. I was and still am heavily into CrossFit and in shape. I had always felt comfortable in the water. The only thing was I didn't realize until I looked to my left and then to my right that I was out there in the open ocean. The swells were very big, so I just kept paddling and really ignored everything else but getting out there.

When I arrived and got closer to this twenty-something-year-old, I could see him trying not to go under. I was about fifty yards away and started to shout out encouragement and direct instructions, like, "It will be okay! Hang in! I will turn the board to the side, and you will grab the side of it." I turned the board to the side and helped him up. The board was in a horizontal position, and he was like a rag doll.

He said, "Thank you! Thank God you came!"

As I turned the board around toward the shore, I realized how freaking far I had come. The people looked like ants. I asked for the kid to help to kick and paddle with one hand, but he was exhausted. At this time, I got a little nervous about all the other things that could happen. I thought of sharks for one second, and then I basically just kept kicking and paddling to shore. Surfside Beach on Nantucket is swim at your own risk; there are no lifeguards. After about thirty to forty minutes, as we approached the shore, people started to help. The kid collapsed and was taken away on a three-wheeler with first responders. People on the shore, at least fifty, were applauding. Some were crying, and I started to vomit a bit and convulsed as the adrenaline was pumping.

"Dan," said Jack, "let's sit down."

I did and drank about ten rum and Cokes after. I must say I did not sleep too well that night, and as a matter of fact, I think about it often and get a bit scared of all the things that could have gone wrong. My kids were young, ten and twelve, and I could tell it was scary for them as well.

The next day, the volleyball games continued, and we happened to be playing against a firefighter from Nantucket. He asked if I was the guy who saved the kid and if I had any special training. I told him I was the guy but had no training. He was shocked. He gave me a high five and was like, "Man, you are the dude!"

Later that summer, we visited a friend's house in Maine, and her parents heard about the story. They also informed me that the same type of thing had happened to them on Nantucket, and their friend went to save someone but ended up drowning. They all had to take the ferry back with a casket on board.

It was the second episode I had had with the water and the risk of drowning. The first happened when I was about seventeen. Two friends and I went to go swimming in a lake by Croton, New York. The current was fast, as it was late spring / early summer. The three of us all went over a waterfall. I remember being pounded by massive amounts of churning water on my back and desperately fighting to get out and up for air. I somehow was spit out and was able to hold on to a log by the wall with my other friend, Tim. We then started to panic, as we could not see Scott. Suddenly, we saw his hand coming out of the water and then going down. This set me in a big panic, and I started to scream to people on the shore sunbathing with their kid, "Help! Help! Help!" Amazingly, they all just watched and were frozen until I yelled, "*Jesus Christ*, someone help!" Suddenly, two guys came running from the top of the hill at the parking lot. I will never forget one's name, Joe Zirbo. He was, I believe, just out of high school, but he was a big guy. They grabbed Scott, who literally was like a rag doll, and hoisted him over the wall to the shore. He did not need CPR but was weak and shaken. The two guys then came to Tim and me and guided us down the river. We had to backtrack up the woods all in bare feet and then swim across the lake. It was a frightening experience. However, as we were kids, we got back in the car and all went home. When our parents asked how the day went, my response was "It all went okay today, about the same."

It is Tuesday, October 27, 2020. We are a week before the national elections, and the country is as divided as ever. I spent my weekend visiting my parents, which I have managed to do over many decades. It happened to be a very special, spontaneous weekend. On Saturday afternoon, my sister texted me to join her and my brother-in-law Steve at a surprise birthday party for our old friend and neighbor Diane. It was a great night, as so many old friends arrived and reconnected. I hadn't seen so many in over thirty years. This group of friends from Ossining knew me when I was very much an out-of-control wise-ass kid who was already way down a bad path, and now they saw what I had accomplished. I couldn't even tell them the whole history. It is way too complex and long.

As I drove back to Franklin from New York, I was reminded of how many worlds I had become part of. The friends from Ossining knew me one way. Then I was in the DR, Massachusetts, and Virginia and have been in Franklin for the past twenty-four years. The old friends still call me Danny, which is pretty funny since that name has left me for over thirty years, excluding my parents of course.

Ellen finished her school and passed her boards. She has done such an amazing job in her new career. We were both working and guiding Austin through the college application process. Both boys have accomplished a great deal at this point. Austin is a senior at Providence College and Carter a sophomore at the University of Massachusetts Amherst. How proud we are as parents of their achievements and how much work we did and how involved we were in helping them achieve their own goals. As we are eight months into COVID-19, the college scene and job market are very tough and not fair, to say the least. However, it is just another example of a situation out of our control. That being said, you just need to keep moving and grinding forward. I hope and pray the boys have the perseverance to get through these most difficult times. Isolation in dorms and off campus living is not easy. Having all their classes online is a complete joke. Austin, the senior, should be having job expos and job fairs for employment opportunities, but it's just not happening, which is so disappointing. This is the hand that has been dealt, and now we all have to adjust. Carter, my youngest, spent many years in the recruiting world for lacrosse. He is now a sophomore at UMass Amherst with his first season cut short, and this season this spring may change in a second. Trying to plug forward and stay motivated in these times is difficult, to say the least. I think about my boys and their generation. They were babies during 9/11; they have seen wars on the TV, terrorism, school shootings, a recession in 2008–2009, and now a pandemic with an entire workforce changing. They will prevail in these difficult times. It is all about adjusting and adapting to the new norms. In some way, I feel we let their generation down.

Chapter 20

Life Goes on at the Clinic

Back at the clinic today, we happened to lose a patient in for a routine neuter. It was an anesthetic death with no rhyme or reason; it just happens in the matter of a second. My associate was about to do the procedure when the dog's heart and breathing stopped. The technicians and entire staff were upset, which is obviously normal. What I needed to remind them of was that this job was not routine; nothing was routine. The consent form that the owner signs doesn't make the guilt and sadness go away. What I try to explain to all is you need to try to compartmentalize these situations. When things are going well, everyone is very happy, but you need to be prepared for the bad things and know how to deal with the unforeseen sad, traumatic situations. Most important is having the will to step back, take a breath, and keep going, little by little.

I try to explain to them they need to take in all the good, positive, rewarding work we do for the clients and their pets. You can't let the random sad things define you or your work. I am not sure where the client will go with this. As an owner, you need to be prepared for a letter from the client's attorney.

Lawsuits and liability are part of this business and many other businesses in this day and age. It never was like this when I started in the mid- to late eighties and through the mid-nineties.

I remember working at Tufts and attending one of the sessions for small animal rounds. One of the clinicians stood up and said, "If you are afraid of being sued, you shouldn't be in the business." Dr. Frank Pipers was right on in one sense, but in another, it is a bit too nonchalant. When the lawsuits come at you, they can take over your entire being. I will give you a list of personal episodes and then go into some others where I needed to intervene, as I chaired the ethics and grievance committee for the state of Massachusetts. I have to repeat myself: I was the chair of this committee. I don't know how I had the time, running the practice. I think back to when I was this wise-ass kid with below-average grades growing up in Ossining, New York.

The first time I was sued, I was about two weeks into my new job here in Franklin in 1996. I received a letter from my previous employer down in South Dartmouth. This was the practice I ran out of or was thrown out of, depending on whom you talk to. There was a case about a month before I left of a pregnant golden retriever with severe ear infections. I saw the dog and prescribed a medication called panolog. It is an ear medication that has antibiotics, antiyeast agents, and cortisone. Weeks later, the mother whelped, but as days went by, one by one, almost all nine pups were dying. It took us two days to realize all the pups were born with cleft palates. When I received the letter from the owners, I started to shake, and my heart was racing. I had just started this new job and had to explain to my new boss I had a lawsuit coming. He gave me the number of an attorney in Franklin. I explained everything, and he sent off a very scathing letter to my former boss, reminding her that being the owner, she was responsible as well. If there were any further issues, she too would be brought into it. The matter ended right there. I guess the claim was that the cortisone could cause cleft palates during pregnancy, but that can be debated until the cows come home. There are many situations of pregnant animals and women for that matter who need cortisone during pregnancy. It was my first experience.

A cat, a dog, and a husband walk into an exam room. Right there, that was trouble. The husband was clueless and was focused on his kids not banging on things while my associate was going over the exams with a mean cat and a very aggressive dog. Long story short, he got home, and they put the dog flea and tick medication on the cat. The cat ended up at the emergency room and was treated and released the next day. The wife called and wanted me to reimburse her a thousand dollars. Looking back, I should have done that. It cost me close to ten thousand getting an attorney and fighting it. It wasn't our fault. However, you have to go through the hoops with the board of the state and prove to all you are not a criminal. The owners got nothing really but just caused us a lot of wasted time and money. The amount of energy it took and stress was too much.

Week after week, month after month, there was another letter coming from their attorney or the board asking for something else. During this time, I was trying to keep a clear head and get through the day. I kept focusing on the next lacrosse game and who would be in my starting lineup.

A German shepherd puppy in an exam room was showing signs of aggression. My associate was feeding him little dog treats to distract him. He was inhaling them, and one got caught in his trachea. Before you know it, he and my other associate were doing CPR and a tracheostomy. I got this news while landing in Logan after a vacation in the DR. After getting all my information in order, I actually spoke directly to the owner. I offered him the cost of the dog and all the fees that they spent over the last three months when they purchased the dog.

It was over five thousand dollars. The cost of business, I guess you can call it. Things have changed since I was sitting at the front desk and answering phones on Sundays, while the old Italian women would bring me food and thank me for all I had done for their pets.

As chairman of the ethics and grievance committee, it was pretty tough watching crazy people try to destroy the reputations of hardworking colleagues. There is no room for human error; that is for sure.

I have two close friends who were humiliated in the media, and that was way before social media. Mark is a good friend of mine who was caring for a small dog with pancreatitis. Against his advice, the owners took the dog home. They refused hospitalization, and the dog died. Lawyers got involved along with the *Boston Herald* and the radio station WBCN. They were accusing him of not caring and not attending to their needs. He lost his reputation, and his place of employment hung him out to dry. They didn't want to stand the heat of the bad press. He was a young vet starting his career and needed to work out of the back of his car for years seeing horses and doing house calls. After years of attorneys and defending his reputation, Mark actually countersued, and later it was revealed that the couple who caused him all this stress were fugitives and wanted for mortgage fraud. Mark is a very successful vet and has a thriving equine practice on the south shore.

Rich is a friend and colleague of mine who has retired. He was on the golf course and was being attacked by crazy aggressive Canada geese. He took his club and protected himself. He knocked the eye out of one of the geese. You would think that this guy was Lucifer himself. His name was all over the news. It was a complete disaster.

I have been the mediator of lawsuits that were so crazy one would question why we were there wasting time. I guess the public realizes once a complaint arrives at the state board, the board has to address the issue. You can identify the real crazy claims, like when the lady's mouse meant everything to her, and her letters would ramble and ramble on about this mouse. It was a complete shit show.

Threats of violence and revenge did happen. I have seen the public change. It is not all negative. I still believe the majority of people are good. I believe in my profession a couple of things have happened. The demands of the public are for sure a big problem. They want their issues attended to and also want immediate results. They assume because 90 percent of them are paying in cash that they should be guaranteed positive solutions. You have to remind them that in health, there are no guarantees. The American public is also much lonelier and more separated from friends and family. Their pets are their family. That has always been the case, but it is multiplied by a thousand now. I have seen the full circle. You will have the couple living together or just married get a dog. They will arrive at the practice weekly if the dog looked left when he should have turned right. That couple is there constantly until they have a baby. When baby arrives, you see them less and less. The young families getting their new pets are always there, and it's the time I really enjoy most. I do like talking to the kids and showing them how to take care of their new pet. The empty-nester couple are next on the list of new pets. They are there constantly and are now trying to figure out how to take care of a new pet and watch the grandchildren.

The elderly are among my favorite clients. This group is the reason why I started a house call practice. They are caring and love their pets. They also appear to be the ones who are most alone. What has happened now is I am seeing the kids of those young families who are now young adults bringing their new pets in and traveling far distances to be at the clinic requesting medical care. This is what they know and are very comfortable with. It all has come full circle in many senses of the word.

So the economic stress of caring for a pet, the loneliness, and the entitlement of wanting guarantees right away have caused a lot of stress in the veterinary field. It again is why the younger generations of vets and staff members are having an extra hard time dealing with it. They have their own economic stress with student loans and are certainly are not allowed to make a mistake in this environment.

About fifteen years ago, one of my associates performed surgery on a German shepherd for an ear hematoma. She did a great job, but the owner was convinced the ear was off two millimeters to the right. I pleaded with this guy that it was fine and even had one of my specialist surgeons say it was all standard procedure. He went off on me on the phone at one point and said, "Dan, you leave me no other options."

I responded, "What are you referring to?"

He came in a month later with the same problem on the other ear. I said, "Look, we will take care of it, but you can't behave like this. Plus you are an intimidating guy, and you are getting the front desk nervous."

He picked up his dog that afternoon with flowers for the front desk. About two weeks later, I heard his name on the news. He had barricaded himself in his basement and came up from the bulkhead with a high-powered rifle with a scope on it. A SWAT team shot and killed him right in Franklin.

I spoke with a professor at Angel Memorial after this incident. Dr. Mike Pavletic is a well-known surgeon. He agreed with my take on the public. He mentioned sometimes when he goes into an exam room, he really doesn't know what these people are thinking and what exactly they have in their backpack. I have excused myself from an exam room and called Franklin Police many times to have someone removed. It is just a threatening vibe you get, and you have to go with your gut instinct.

During my internship at Iowa State, I and a couple of the residents were doing the overnight in ICU. We all were exchanging crazy stories of the public. I brought up how the owners of a boxer were freebasing cocaine and were blowing it into the dog's face. He eventually died a sudden death. That was when I first started in Staten Island, New York. One of the residents mentioned that every Fourth of July, he received a letter from a crazy client saying that this was the anniversary of when he killed his dog.

Chapter 21

Curbside Treatment—In the Era of COVID-19

We have had a steady run of colleagues and employees at the practice for many years now even with all the ups and downs—especially during these last eight months since the pandemic hit in March of 2020. The practice has succeeded and excelled in these difficult times. When COVID-19 first started, all were in a panic, rightly so. I just kept telling the staff, "We will go day to day and not make any major or reactionary decisions." If you want to stay home, then go ahead, but we will stay open. We adjusted to the times and created and became very efficient in curbside treatment. This means owners are not allowed inside in order to maintain social distancing. We noticed that the pets that were more dominant or aggressive were less so without the owners. We also realized that the majority of the public liked it better as well. It was less stressful for the owner to come in with the pets and most of the time multiple kids. In other words, the curbside treatment is here to stay and will be modified as we adjust.

I think this demeanor is part of me now. It is what I needed to do my whole life. I don't get caught up with things we don't have. If the computer is down, so what? Let me see the next dog. If the electricity goes out, well, I studied many nights by candlelight. There is something that I have developed over the years to not sweat the small stuff. What? You took a loan out for $1.3 million and two years later you took another one out for another $1 million? Don't sweat it. You can't take it with you, and you just need to keep plugging, practicing medicine, and all the numbers will fall into place, as Dr. Tom Carreras told me so many years ago.

At that time, in 1986, he was just starting his practice. Remember that was the time he asked me to heat his coffee up in a microwave, and I was so Dominicanized, I didn't even know how to work a microwave.

Chapter 22

The Veterinary Industry, Corporate versus Private

The veterinary industry has been taken over by the major corporations. These are corporations that pay the owner in cash, ask the owner to stay on board for a while, and then have the suits or managers run the practice. This sounds way too familiar, and it reminds me of how the corporation took over my dad's workplace in Ossining, Stony Lodge. It was a complete disaster. Not to say it's all bad, but my goal was to avoid doing that and to perhaps sell part of the practice within.

The majority of veterinarians are not willing to take it on for multiple reasons. The financial aspect is number one. It is a lot of money and a lot of responsibility, and not many are willing to go to that level. About three years ago, I started to have some open discussion with one of my associates, Dr. Sara Gray. She has been with me for about eleven years now. She is a perfect prospect for ownership and has the full package. She doesn't take things too seriously, is great with clients, and most important, is great with staff. She also happens to be a very good veterinarian and a very good surgeon. There is one thing she doesn't have, and that is money. This sounds very familiar, but my approach with her is going to be much different than what it was for me when I did my buy-in, buyout in 2002. I have lent her a page from my playbook. No need for money, Sara, we will find it and make it happen. On another note, women are now and have been for decades the dominant force in the veterinary profession. However, they are not in the majority when it comes to practice ownership. It's now time for a change, and the future of the Franklin Veterinary Clinic will be in good hands. Sara was also pregnant and raised an infant while in veterinary school; multitasking and stress management are second nature.

First and foremost, I am honest, and I don't bullshit anyone. I lay it out on the line. This may be a fault, but it is what it is. Could I have offered the practice to one of the corporations that call almost weekly and make percentages more on the deal? Yes, absolutely, but that is not me. I have been with many in this work family for twenty years now. When I say percentages more, we are talking about possible hundreds of thousands more over a period of time. I offered Sara this proposal, a gradual buy-in over ten years. This would be part of my exit strategy. I feel this will work for not only the both of us but the entire staff and community of Franklin. It will be the continuity of the culture of the practice for our clients and staff.

After a year of preparation and dealing, we signed an agreement on August 30, 2018. The difference was and is that I made it happen and helped her. I am providing her the opportunity like my former boss did with me but in a much different way. It's amazing the practice that I bought in 2002 for $800,000 has now tripled. One doesn't think of the growth. It just happens as you are in the trenches day in and day out. It reminds me of the words my old boss Tom Carreras used to say, "Just keep working and practicing good medicine, and the numbers will fall in place." The key is that these are all goals and plans, but remember what I said about goals and plans. They are good to have and better when achieved, but you need to realize that plans and goals may change, and you need to adjust. Sara will succeed, and my goal is to make that happen. She is awesome, and the team is all in place to continue. Her issue will be her success.

It is quite remarkable that it doesn't seem that long ago when I was taking the CPE exam in Starkville, Mississippi. I was hanging with a couple of the students in a bar after the exam and hoping I had enough money in my pocket to buy a round of drinks for the small group. I remember when I was in Iowa, living in a hotel room, eating yogurt and canned tuna daily, waiting for a check from Sydell on a monthly basis. I was completely broke. And when my close friend asked me if owned a credit card, I said no and then applied for one. I was given a card through Citibank with a three-hundred-dollar credit limit. I also remember moving to Worcester with a hole in the floor of the car and sleeping in a shit apartment on the floor for two weeks until I could afford a bed. What has happened transpired through confidence, risk taking, and not taking any shit from anyone. Look what has been accomplished.

I never gauge success for anyone on the money they generate or materialistic things. However, look what has happened in less than eighteen years when I took a loan out from the back of a veterinary journal for $125,000. Remember the ten-year loan at 10 percent interest that had no balloon payment? It was $1,727 per month for ten years.

Chapter 23

Good Debt versus Bad Debt

Think about it. The house we bought for $604,000 in 2004 is paid off. It is now worth possibly $750,000 to $800,000. The building of the clinic that I bought in 2002 for $450,000 is worth well over $1.5 million and will be paid off soon. In 2013, I purchased the property next to the clinic for $450,000 with no money down but used the clinic as collateral. I completely renovated it, and now it is used for parking for the twenty-plus employees and is also part of a rental income from the two apartments. It will be paid off very soon. It's worth maybe $700,000.

In 2015, I purchased an apartment in La Romana for $160,000 through my contacts with my family. I get some income through Airbnb and use it when I can. Unfortunately, with COVID, it has been struggling. Now I just need the Airbnb to help pay monthly expenses. This month, a year ago, on November 22, Ellen and I closed on a house on Cape Cod. It's about an hour and fifteen minutes from our home in Franklin. We were vacationing on the Cape last summer, and I needed to head back to work for some surgeries. I was able to head back and return that afternoon and be on the beach. I thought to myself, *Well, this is not a bad deal*, and decided to take the money from the first buy-in and put it to work on a house. We started to look that late August into September, and before we knew it, we were closing in November 2019. I pulled out all the stops—of course with Walter's advice.

The house went for $879,000, so I offered $779,000. We eventually paid $810,000. I had the down payment but did what I started to get good at. Get to the head of the line if you want the house. Say no contingencies. I don't have to sell anything to buy it.

Say you will pay in cash! That is a real attention getter. In the meantime, I have no cash! The bank has the cash. Through Walter, I was able to get a loan for interest only for seven years at 3.5 percent. I am paying less for that house than it cost for my initial ten-year loan at 10 percent that I got in the back of a magazine. For some reason, with COVID, the market on the Cape has exploded. The value of that house is a lot more than what I paid for it, and I will have no mortgage in the next year or two.

I bring these purchases to your attention in no way to brag. As a matter of fact, most people don't even know the details. First, I spent the last twenty-five years in a lot of debt that many would not be comfortable with. Debt, by the way, people all around me said I was too crazy to take on. Through hard work and discipline, it is all starting to be paid off. I would say this, for the people who don't know me and look at me as the wealthy practice owner, they have no clue what the fuck they are talking about. The people who think that I was given this or perhaps I was from money and that's how I accomplished these assets have no clue what they are talking about. The people or even family members who think I had it easy going to the DR and then getting licensed, and, wow, look what happened overnight, do not know the details. These are the things that can get you irritated, but I learned to ignore them. This is all based on hard work, stubbornness, and working harder than others because I perhaps didn't feel I was as smart as they were. I locked myself up in a room and worked around the clock from 1981 in vet school until I was licensed in 1992.

With all of these accomplishments, I still enjoy what I am doing. I am in and out of the practice with my work family day in and day out through these most stressful times, providing service for the families in and around Franklin who have become close on a personal level through these years.

How do you explain to someone that my class rank in high school was 374 out of 420? My GPA was 74.6? My SAT was 200 and 300, and then I got the same grades when I repeated the test. Yet I made it in one of the most competitive and difficult professions there is. I started at the age of eighteen in a different country being taught in a different language, having to take a tape recorder to school and listen to it at night, at times by candlelight. All are capable of achieving what they want. You just need to make the personal decision to *do it* and not worry about anyone else or get distracted.

Now I have put myself in a position where the banks want to keep loaning me money. I try to tell the younger people a couple of things that are important and I think are what made me somewhat marketable to banks. The first thing is to be patient. There is no rush, assuming you have to achieve all of your goals by the time you leave college at the age of twenty-two. You can set goals, but you need to be patient. Everyone is looking for a quick deal, which is fine, but you need to have passion and the drive for what you want. You certainly cannot be caught up on other opinions from family and friends. If you want something, you do need to be determined to get it and be prepared to fail. As far as a business goes, I am old school, and I feel it is as true now as ever before, which differentiates me and this practice from the corporations. We build it on relationships. It is the reason why clients and now their kids travel many miles to come our practice. From a business point of view, you offer them a service and build trust over time. That return on investment is worth every penny. Why pressure a client and their pet to do all the tests or procedures at once and whack them for a large amount of money? They may never come back again, and sometimes it's just not warranted. You will generate more over a period of years and trust providing a service than you would if you were only to see someone once or twice. Client retention is the key. As you build the culture, the entire team has to be on board or buy into the philosophy.

I have always had very good credit. Whenever I had a bill, I paid it. I never missed any payment of any bill ever, including credit cards. It's funny, at one time, I had a credit limit of $300, and now I have monthly credit card bills of $75,000 to $100,000. I always pay my bills and never play any games. I am consistent with this in every respect. Whether it's vendors, drug companies, products, or even contractors, I pay everyone. If I hire a contractor and we have a deal and he or she does the work, that's it; he or she gets paid.

You can't be afraid of the numbers or debt, and you need to know the difference between good debt and bad debt. I never was afraid of debt or owing money. I knew that things could change in a second. I bring this up only because a sudden change of circumstances had a huge effect on me. September 11 was an event that changed everything. You can be in an office one second starting your day with a cup of coffee, and a freaking plane comes crashing through the window. Then you have to decide to either burn or jump. After a tragedy like this, everything else is secondary. The banks will get their money one way or another. Don't get me wrong. I owe the banks that I have worked with and their relationships a lot of gratitude. They took a chance on me, and the relationship has always been a two-way street. The systems in our country have provided me a chance to succeed. I say this realizing that for others, the systems aren't so fair.

A good debt is a house or maybe a business that you can sell. Real estate to me is good debt. Bad debt would be a boat, unless you have the money to pay for it in cash. Taking a loan out for a boat may not be the smartest thing to do, especially if you are carrying other debt on houses or other investments that are keeping you from banking some cash.

I think about how little I had at certain times through this journey. My wife, Ellen, was a big part of more than half of the journey, and I owe her everything. She did all the heavy lifting, staying at home with the boys, who were born eighteen months apart. She has now created her new journey, going back to school and working in her new successful career as a respiratory therapist. It wasn't easy at all from the beginning with the two us. As a matter of fact, I didn't even have enough money for an engagement ring, and we never had a honeymoon. Our first date was at the Piccadilly Pub in Westborough, Massachusetts, because the pitchers of beer were cheap. She has stood by me and no doubt created a sense of stability. There is no way all of this could have happened if it wasn't for her and the stability of the family.

I often think about what this profession provided not only me and my own family but also the people, staff and clients, who have made this happen. I was not only able to afford for Ellen to go back to school but for the boys to go to a private high school, a boarding school, and very good colleges. Now it is up to the boys to make their own journey, but I don't want them to struggle the way I did. There is no need for it, and life is too short. This is my choice, and some may disagree. They are both working very hard with a very uncertain future dealing with this COVID-19 pandemic. They are off campus, taking classes online, and perhaps going into a very different workforce.

The staff themselves have become a family. Some have come and gone, and some have returned. Some have been with me for long while, and I do love them. Sometimes we argue or get mad at each other, just like you would in any other type of family. Welcome to the family, welcome to a little dysfunction here and there. It's all part of life, and we are all just trying to get through it, one day at a time. Even with all the uncertainty with COVID and the social and political unrest, it's all about getting through things day by day. For me and I believe for many of us, we all have to get up and get to work the next day. So I try to tell most people, "Don't get caught up in the hype. Just keep moving and keep working."

I often think about my next act. As I mentioned in the beginning, I started my journey to become a veterinarian at the age of eighteen. I am fifty-eight years old now! Wow, that is a long time, forty years! This is all I know, and I really don't know how to do anything else. I really can't retire for another eight years or so. I would be about sixty-six years of age. I can stay in the field or perhaps think of something different, but I do believe I would like to have an impact on people and things. Working with or influencing kids is a possibility. I would work with them all, whether going to their schools or coaching or perhaps helping the young kids who are going down the wrong path or teaching. I think that may be the most impactful. I know one thing I will never do, and that is to become a handyman putzing around the house. I was never good with my hands and don't have the interest or patience, but I am truly amazed by builders and contractors on what they do and create. I have become friendly with so many, so if anything needs to be done, I can always call on them. I most likely will stay in the field in some way, whether it's shelter work or continuing to work with the Vet Dogs. These are the dogs trained by prisoners and then offered to the wounded warriors. We have been involved with the program since the beginning, over fifteen years now. I actually was able to get a tour of the prison in Framingham. I learned a lot from the warden. She mentioned that she wished all citizens could have the opportunity to tour. What I got out of it is if it weren't for alcohol, drugs, and some bad decisions, the prison population would be cut in half. Just my opinion.

I know one thing that I am very good at, and that is relaxing, sitting on the beach with a cooler and reading or listening to music, but I'm always reflecting and thinking of the next move. Lately, I have been thinking of a hobby for my next chapter. It is something that falls into the category of bad debt, and that is boating. As mentioned before, it's bad debt if you are unable to afford it, and that won't be the issue. It's never about how much money you have; it's how much you owe. With luck, hard work, and shrewd moves, I have been able to chip away at large sums of debt.

It is not fair to say that all of what I accomplished I created on my own without help from others, but it is true that nothing of this was given to me. It is all self-made. I do reflect and think of the people along the way, the good people who were encouraging. I remember teachers from the time I was young in Brookside School and middle school, including Judy Beherns, Joe Variano, and Charles Hines, and the teacher in the Dominican Republic who helped me every Saturday for almost a year after I got a sixteen on my first biology test. I also think of my parents and family in the Dominican Republic who took me in as their own for six years and the number of times I had my bags packed and was ready to give it all up but they encouraged me to keep moving forward. I remember my family on Staten Island, like my aunt Sissy, who sent me money to pay for an exam without me even asking, and my aunt Mary, who introduced me to the books by author James Herriot (*All Creatures Great and Small*). I think of Tom Carreras, who paid me $3.35 an hour after vet school but really drilled into me the work ethic and how to think like a clinician; my dear friend who sent so many letters of encouragement while I was in the DR; her mom, who gave me that hug and whispered words like "Work hard, and you can do it" when at that time all thought it was impossible; Bob Murtaugh, who listened to my story, sat back at his desk, and said, "I don't know what it is about you, Dan, but you will persevere"; the good people at Iowa State and in Virginia, including the Katz family, who as tragic as that situation was, believed in me and gave me confidence; and the community of Franklin and the surrounding towns, who have instilled their trust in me and our staff day in and day out.

These are the things that make you continue to move forward in a positive way. The staff who have come in day in and day out for many years are the ones who for sure make it possible. Their hard work and dedication make it all possible. For them, I also owe a debt of gratitude.

I can't tell my story in a minute or two. It's too long and diverse, but I do believe it is very interesting. It is a story of trauma to me personally as well to some very close friends. Think about it. At my first job as a veterinarian, which I got at the age of thirty, my boss's son committed suicide, and I was cleaning his blood off the carpet and seeing clients the same day. I was with him the night before so excited about the 1992 presidential election. Six months later, his mother, my boss, also committed suicide. Five years later, there was a murder-suicide with two close friends. Three years ago, my mentor and very good friend Dr. Peter

Kintzer, the one who advised me about Iowa, left his house one morning, and a tree was uprooted and killed him while he was driving to work five minutes from his house. He was at my practice almost weekly consulting. I have text messages with him from the day before he was killed, planning his next visit. Ironically, his daughter Zoe jumped on board in the practice three years ago and now is starting her own family. Life is constantly changing and moving forward.

So I take the next chapter in some ways with a grain of salt. I plan but realize there may be another plan for me at any given time. I wake up each day grateful and realize what a gift every day is and what an incredible journey it has been. I hope you all enjoyed it.

Persevere, and move forward.

CPSIA information can be obtained
at www.ICGtesting.com
Printed in the USA
BVHW031641240821
615125BV00014B/963/J